THE
WAGES
OF SIN

Wisconsin Studies in Film

David Bordwell
Donald Crafton
Vance Kepley, Jr.
Kristin Thompson

General Editors

THE WAGES
OF SIN

CENSORSHIP AND THE
FALLEN WOMAN FILM
1928–1942

Lea Jacobs

The University of Wisconsin Press

The University of Wisconsin Press
114 North Murray Street
Madison, Wisconsin 53715

3 Henrietta Street
London WC2E 8LU, England

Printed in the United States of America

    A section of Chapter 1 was published in a somewhat different form in *Home Is Where the Heart Is: Studies in Melodrama and the Woman's Film,* ed. Christine Gledhill (London: British Film Institute, 1987). A version of chapter 5 was originally published in *Cinema Journal* 27, no. 3 (1988). Portions of Chapters 1, 2, and 5 appeared in *The Velvet Light Trap* 23 (1989). Reprinted from *The Velvet Light Trap,* Number 23, Spring 1989 by permission of the University of Texas Press.
    Publicity stills from *Susan Lenox* and *The Easiest Way* are reproduced by permission of the Turner Entertainment Co. Copyright © 1931 Metro-Goldwyn-Mayer Distributing Corporation, copyright renewed 1958 Loew's Inc.
    Publicity stills from *Our Dancing Daughters* and *The Greeks Had a Word for Them* are reproduced courtesy of Wisconsin Center for Film and Theater Research.

Library of Congress Cataloging-in-Publication Data
Jacobs, Lea.
    The wages of sin : censorship and the fallen woman film,
1928–1942 / Lea Jacobs.
        214 pp.   cm. —(Wisconsin studies in film)
        Includes bibliographical references and index.
        1. Motion pictures—Censorship—United States—History.   2. Women
    in motion picutres.   3. Sex in motion pictures.   I. title.
    II. Series.
    PN1995.62.J3   1991
    791.43'082 —dc20
    ISBN 0-229-12880-6   90-50647
    ISBN 0-299-12884-9 (pbk.)   CIP

For Rosalia and David Jacobs,
my first, and best, teachers

CONTENTS

PREFACE

In John Stahl's *Back Street,* the mistress of a married man helps him to achieve fame and fortune while remaining discreetly in the background of his life. Submissive and supportive, she makes sacrifices for her lover and remains with him until his death. She is a "perfect," if not legally sanctioned, wife. In the early thirties, this film occasioned much correspondence between Universal Studio and Lamar Trotti of the Motion Picture Producers and Distributors Association, the trade association responsible for industry self-censorship. The film was condemned by the Catholic Legion of Decency in 1934 during the time when the Legion threatened a boycott of the industry. And, in the late thirties, industry censors insisted that Universal Studio remake the film rather than re-release the Stahl version.[1]

This case sparked my interest in the history of censorship. After viewing the film, I could not comprehend why *Back Street* had been so controversial. Although the film portrayed an unmarried couple, it celebrated an idea of romantic love, and lifelong, faithful (and for the woman monogamous) union. Moreover, its tone was extremely subdued. There were no passionate love scenes, and, in comparison with the original novel, only the most discreet references to the heroine's status as mistress or kept woman.

The problem, then, was a historical one: to reconstruct the grounds on which this film had been defined and experienced as offensive. And this was a question not simply of sexual explicitness, but of the systems of characterization and narrative development considered necessary in films dealing with adultery. The main problem with *Back Street,* according to industry censors, was precisely that the heroine appeared so meek and unobjectionable, and that her love affair, which censors regarded as "sinful," was favorably compared with a legal marriage. Extending the terms of this argument, I would suggest that the film would have been deemed less offensive if the love affair had been steamier or the heroine's motives more venal, that is, if the affair had been more clearly marked as transgressive.

The controversy over *Back Street* suggests the difficulty of explaining censorship simply as an attempt to remove illicit sex or violence from films. While censors did not actually suggest putting sex "into" the story of a kept woman, the logic of their criticisms led in that direction. More precisely, the problem posed by the film was not content per se but rather the narrative construction which seemed to direct the spectator's sympathy for the heroine.

In my view, the case of *Back Street* is quite typical of the operations of industry self-censorship in the thirties. Industry censors and producers treated proscribed ideas as problems of narrative and film form. To understand censorship, then, we need to reconstruct the institutional framework within which these problems were identified and solutions suggested.

I propose to reconstruct this institutional framework by examining a genre which posed some distinct problems for the MPPDA—the fallen woman film. In the thirties, in the course of conflict between the film industry and various reform groups, this genre was singled out as "the kept woman story" or more commonly "the sex picture." Like the gangster film with which it was sometimes compared, the fallen woman film served as a focal point for public criticism of the film industry. As a consequence of such criticism, it was targeted for regulation by the MPPDA.

These films concern a woman who commits a sexual transgression such as adultery or premarital sex. In traditional versions of the plot, she is expelled from the domestic space of the family and undergoes a protracted decline. Alone on the streets, she becomes an outcast, often a prostitute, suffering various humiliations which usually culminate in her death. In other variants of the story, however, the movement away from the family does not lead to a decline in class. Instead the heroine, a stereotypical "kept woman" or "gold digger," uses men to become rich.

The fallen woman film offers a fruitful example for the study of industry self-regulation because such films helped to define the limits of what was permissible, especially in the realm of sexuality. Many of the MPPDA's rules for handling stories which involved so-called sexual deviance were elaborated specifically in terms of this genre. Further, the successive instances of the fallen woman film can be seen as attempts to work on and around the rules of the genre in an effort to render potentially offensive stories acceptable. The focus upon a genre thus permits us systematically to trace out the permutations of narrative conventions instigated by censorship.

The fallen woman film permits us to examine not only the operations of censorship under the studio system, but more specifically, the representation of sexual difference within this context. Much recent feminist theory and criticism has been concerned with the ways in which the classical Hollywood film constructed received notions of the feminine. Such constructions were explicitly at issue in efforts to regulate the fallen woman film. Reformers, industry censors, and producers engaged in prolonged debates about how to bolster normative definitions of gender roles, marriage, and family life within the constraints of the genre. This proved to be difficult in several notorious cases—which I will call limit texts—in which censors approved and released films that were subsequently condemned by groups such as the Catholic Legion of Decency and state censorship agencies. These "failures" on the part of industry censors provide interesting cases for feminist criticism, in that they indicate how films which seemingly observed the sexual status quo could simultaneously call it into question.

In seeking out cases indicative of the lapses of censorship, this study necessarily raises questions of periodization. Historians have traditionally made a distinction between the early thirties (1930–33), when industry self-censorship was weak or ineffective, and the late thirties (after 1934), when censorship became more powerful. During the years 1933 and 1934, pressure by the Catholic Legion of Decency and other reform groups necessitated the elaboration of more extensive regulatory mechanisms for the protection of the industry. While I shall argue against the generally accepted explanation of this change as a strict "enforcement" of the industry's Production Code, this study retains the emphasis upon 1934 as a turning point in the administration of industry self-regulation. By comparing cases from before and after 1934, I propose to analyze differences in the treatment of the fallen woman genre under the two administrations of censorship.

Chapter 1 discusses the social pressures which led the MPPDA to single out the fallen woman film, among other genres, for censorship. It also seeks to explain the ways the MPPDA responded to these social pressures, through a process of negotiation between producers and industry censors over specific films and scripts. The argument then turns to the examination of six cases, selected from a representative sample of one hundred fallen woman films reviewed by MPPDA officials. Chapters 2, 3, and 4 discuss cases from the early thirties, while Chapters 5 and 6 analyze those from the latter part of the decade. Each case study encompasses a review of materials held within the MPPDA censorship files, including treatments, revised portions of scripts, and the correspondence written by industry censors.

I am grateful to the Wisconsin Center for Film and Theater Research for a Rockefeller Fellowship which gave me the opportunity to complete this project. Many people have been most generous in providing access to documents. Mr. Al Van Schmus, formerly of the Motion Picture Producers Association, and Sam Gill, of the Margaret Herrick Library at the Academy of Motion Picture Arts and Sciences, were instrumental in preserving the censorship case files and making them available for research. Michael Friend, Eddie Richmond, of the UCLA Film and Television Archives, and Maxine Fleckner-Ducey, of the Wisconsin Center for Film and Theater Research, helped me to see many obscure films from the thirties.

I initiated this study as a doctoral student at UCLA. I benefited from lengthy and pleasurable conversations with my advisor, Janet Bergstrom, concerning models of the classical text. The section of this study on Joseph von Sternberg is indebted to her work on German emigré directors. Dana Polan encouraged me in this, as in so many other projects. Nataša Ďurovičová and Charles Wolfe patiently read the many drafts of this study and, as always, asked all the right questions. David Bordwell, Janet Staiger, and Kristin Thompson's research on film style and the mode of production has pointed the way to source materials and suggested new ways of thinking about the Hollywood studio system. I particularly want to thank my editor, Kristin Thompson, and David Bordwell for their telling criticisms of this book and great personal kindness. Ben Brewster, as good a copy editor as he is a cook, brightened the final months of revision.

THE
WAGES
OF SIN

1

The Fallen Woman Film and the Impetus for Censorship

The important thing is to leave the audience with the definite conclusion that immorality is not justifiable, that society is not wrong in demanding certain standards of its women, and that the guilty woman, through realization of her error, does not tempt other women in the audience to follow her course.

JASON JOY, *industry censor*

IN THIS ADVICE, written to Columbia's Harry Cohn, the MPPDA official Jason Joy anticipated and sought to forestall some of the objections typically raised against Hollywood movies in the thirties.[1] Reformers argued that films exercised a pernicious influence upon women. Hollywood was held to be in violation of what one reformer called "the current moral code," to undermine normative definitions of femininity and to promote crime or promiscuity.

Present-day histories of film censorship typically allude to this controversy by using the example of Mae West. Notorious for wisecracks and sexual innuendo, West is said to have generated negative publicity for Hollywood and contributed to the institution of stricter mechanisms of film censorship in the mid-thirties.[2] But the publicity which surrounded West's films and persona formed only one part of a more general discussion about how films might possibly affect sexual mores and conduct. In my view, the pressure on the industry to regulate representations of sexuality is best understood as a function of a set of assumptions about spectatorship, specifically female spectatorship, current in the thirties. I will argue that these assumptions were brought to the forefront of public debate by a particular genre—the fallen woman film.

The criticism of Hollywood framed in terms of how films might affect women began as early as the teens, and varied according to the manner in which spectatorship itself was conceptualized. At the most literal

3

level, newspapers and magazines depicted Hollywood as a cause and potential site of female delinquency—luring girls away from their homes and into a tenuous and morally suspect profession. A number of news stories about the "movie-struck girl" circulated in the popular press in the teens. The stories, often written in the form of a warning to the reader, described the fate of young women who left home and went to Hollywood to pursue an acting career. Unable to find work, encountering only indifference from the studios, or worse, a producer of dubious morals, hundreds of girls were supposedly stranded in Los Angeles.[3] *Photoplay* regularly ran features advising fans of the difficulty of obtaining work in Hollywood and on the daunting skills required to be an actress or film extra.[4]

Most of the films of the twenties adopt a cautionary tone similar to the print media in dealing with the stereotype of the movie-struck girl. An early example of the type is Maurice Tourneur's *A Girl's Folly* (1917). An innocent country girl is encouraged to break into the movies by a handsome matinee idol. She leaves home in expectation of finding work at the movie studio, but fails her screen test and is left without any source of income. Only the appearance of her mother saves her from ruin at the hands of the star. The *American Film Institute Catalog* of feature films from the twenties lists several other examples of melodramas in which a girl goes to Hollywood to seek her fortune, only to become vulnerable to the attentions of an unscrupulous actor, producer, or "sheik." Examples include *Mary of the Movies* (Columbia Productions, 1923), *Broken Hearts of Hollywood* (Warner Brothers, 1926), and *Stranded* (Sterling Pictures, 1927). In a more comic vein, the heroine of *Are Parents People?* (1925) attempts to reunite her estranged parents by pretending to be "moviemad" and to run away with a sheik, star of "The Love Brute." In *Ella Cinders* (1926), the eponymous heroine escapes from the tyranny of her mother and sisters by winning an acting contest and going off to Hollywood. No job is waiting for her at the studio, and she inadvertently causes mayhem on several sets, but eventually she is given a chance and becomes a star. Even when these films exculpate Hollywood as an industry, they indicate that the film producers felt the need to respond to public anxiety about the movie-struck girl. Indeed, the film industry trade association, the MPPDA, was so concerned about this issue that in 1925, in association with the YWCA, it organized a residence for young women seeking work as film actresses.[5]

The rather sensationalized stories about the fate of women in Hollywood were paralleled by a more abstract, and scientifically respectable, discourse on the psychological effects and social consequences of film viewing. The Payne Fund Studies, published in 1933, provide a good example of this kind of analysis of media effects. Although most of the studies dealt with the effects of film viewing on young children, one monograph focused upon male and female adolescents. This study, Herbert Blumer and Philip M. Hauser's *Movies, Delinquency and Crime*, explicitly linked the gangster film with the problem of violent crime among boys in the urban tenements, and the "sex picture"—stories about gold diggers, flappers, and vamps—with delinquency and various forms of prostitution among young women.[6] The following question, part of a survey administered by Blumer and Hauser to girls in reform school, indicates some of the assumptions they made about the effects of film viewing: "Did the movies suggest to you any of the following ideas of making easy money? By getting a job and working. By shoplifting. By 'gold-digging men.' By gambling. By sexual delinquency with men. By living with a man and letting him support you."[7] The responses charted out for girls in this survey question recapitulate many of the complaints about the movies which were being made by other reform groups in the period. Women's clubs, educators, and even some newspaper editors considered the movies a possible cause of "vice."[8]

While reformers and social scientists did not usually describe films in any detail, their discussions of female spectatorship frequently made reference to a genre which I call the fallen woman film.[9] While the genre is not popular with present-day audiences, it was a staple of Hollywood melodrama. Precisely because it was already recognized as a type, however loosely defined, it functioned as a lightning rod, channeling reformers' more general anxieties about Hollywood's effect on sexual mores. Moreover, because the fallen woman story turned upon an act of seduction or adultery, it thematized many of the reformers' own concerns about sexual deviance among female spectators. An overview of these recognized genre conventions will help to make clear how the films came to be perceived as transgressive.

Literary Antecedents

The story of the fallen woman derives from a set of nineteenth-century narrative and iconographic conventions which were themselves in flux in the twenties and early thirties. Traditional renderings of the story, in which the erring woman was irredeemably punished, had begun to seem outdated, at least for some sectors of the audience. For example, in a review of the 1929 version of *Madame X, Variety* warned its readers that the film might not appeal to urban audiences nor to younger viewers: " 'Madame X' should show other than in the metropolises and the keys before it is determined by the film buyers if there is mass appeal in it. The younger element nowadays doesn't want this kind of sex, for the sex angle here is of the sordid sort, the thorough-bred woman going down the line to become an absinthe wretch."[10] Hollywood both solicited and helped to construct the change in audience tastes to which *Variety* refers. The fallen woman story underwent decided transformations early in the postwar period, transformations which were sometimes foregrounded in films about changing sexual mores. In *Wine of Youth* (1924), for example, a young flapper's rather wild and freewheeling style of courtship is misconstrued by her conservative father as a sign of her "ruin." I will argue that the resistance to the fallen woman film on the part of censors and reformers largely centered upon such new permutations of the genre. That is, I will explain the hostile reception of the films in terms of their deviations from the traditions of nineteenth-century melodrama.

The stereotype of the fallen woman pervaded nineteenth-century popular culture, appearing in fiction, stage melodrama, opera, and narrative painting, in British, American, and European contexts. A prototypical example is a set of three paintings by Augustus Egg exhibited in 1858 without titles and now known as *Past and Present*.[11] The first painting is set in a well-appointed drawing room. The accused woman lies prostrate before her husband; in the background two girls are playing, building a house of cards. The second painting is set in a poor and rather bare apartment. The children of the absent mother, now older and alone, stare out the window at the moon and a wisp of cloud. In the last painting, the repetition of the moon and clouds indicates that the scene is simultaneous with the previous one. The woman is beneath the arches of a bridge, an icon traditionally connected to the moment of the fallen woman's isolation and suicide.[12] She is poorly dressed and alone except for a baby (by convention illegitimate) which is barely visible in the frame. Her fall is enacted in this movement from the bourgeois drawing room to the bridge by the river, implying a loss of both class and familial status.

Another variant of the fall concentrates on a young servant, seamstress, or uneducated village girl who is seduced by an upper-class man. In examples of this type, which include works as diverse as Elizabeth Gaskell's *Ruth* (1853), and Thomas Hardy's *Tess of the d'Urbervilles*

(1891), class difference highlights the woman's defenselessness, her status as victim in a system she does not control.[13] Typically, she does not actively desire the rake who pursues her and is unaware of his designs.

In England, stories about errant mothers separated from their children or innocent servant girls seduced and abandoned were a commonplace of both serialized magazine fiction and the novel between 1835 and 1880.[14] Authors of domestic novels such as Elizabeth Inchbald, Amelia Opie, and Elizabeth Helm[15] dealt with the fallen woman, as did many of the major novelists of the period: Anthony Trollope (*Can You Forgive Her?* 1865; *The Vicar of Bullhampton*, 1870), George Eliot (*Adam Bede*, 1859), Wilkie Collins (*The Fallen Leaves*, 1879; *The New Magdalen*, 1873), and George Moore (*Esther Waters*, 1894). In America, two early domestic novels, Susanna Rowson's *Charlotte Temple* (1794) and Hannah Webster Forster's *The Coquette* (1797) treat the type.[16] The fallen woman also plays a central role in Eugène Sue's *Les Mystères de Paris* (1842–43), and, in a more realistic mode, Gustave Flaubert's *Madame Bovary* (1857). The courtesan, a more cynical and knowing version of the type, goes back at least as far as Abbé Prévost's *Manon Lescaut* (1753), but acquired particular notoriety with Zola's *Nana* (1879). The courtesan is redeemed by love in Balzac's *Splendeurs et misères des courtisanes*, in *La Comédie humaine* (1846), and Alexandre Dumas's play *La Dame aux camélias* (1852) from his novel of the same name.

The fallen woman story also provided source material for many well-known opera libretti and stage melodramas. Giuseppi Verdi's *La Traviata* (1853) derives from *La Dame aux camélias*, and Jules Massenet's *Manon* (1885) and Giacomo Puccini's *Manon Lescaut* (1893) from the Prévost novel. There were three stage versions of Mrs. Henry Wood's best-selling novel about an errant mother, *East Lynne* (1861). The play consistently attracted large audiences, becoming one of the standbys to which stock companies reverted when theater revenues were down.[17]

Despite its popularity, the fallen woman story attracted controversy throughout the nineteenth century and was subject to various forms of censorship. Lord Chief Justice Campbell urged enactment of the Obscene Publications Act in England in 1857 after becoming incensed by the English translation of Dumas's *La Dame aux camélias*.[18] In the mid-Victorian period, novels such as Mrs. Gaskell's *Ruth* engendered debate insofar as they represented rape or seduction in a popular medium which found its way into the home.[19] Mudie's circulating library, one of the major distributors of three-volume novels, refused to carry

Eliot's *Adam Bede* and Hardy's *Tess of the d'Urbervilles*.[20] Perhaps the most notorious instance of censorship is the attempted prosecution of Gustave Flaubert in 1857 on the grounds that *Madame Bovary* was offensive to public morals.[21] While not the object of official censure, the second half of *Nana* had to be bowdlerized for serial publication in the journal *Le Voltaire*.[22]

The fallen woman genre consistently offended nineteenth-century readers because plot conventions ran afoul of normative definitions of femininity. Although there has recently been some question about the degree to which individuals adhered to the norm of chastity in practice, as an ideal, purity was central to the Victorian conception of womanhood, at least for the middle class.[23] The genre became problematic insofar as the sympathetic portrayal of the heroine seemed to undermine the distinction between chaste and unchaste women.

The controversies around the genre intensified toward the end of the nineteenth century under the impetus of a number of works which explicitly questioned the moral value of purity. These works, considered daring by contemporary readers, prepared the way for the updated variants of the fallen woman plot which became popular in film and fiction after World War I. In George Moore's *Esther Waters* (1894), the heroine denounces characters who condemn her for having an illegitimate child and struggles to raise her son on meager earnings as a domestic. She finally returns to live with the attractive gambler who seduced her rather than marry a minister. George Bernard Shaw's play *Mrs. Warren's Profession* (1894) also inverts traditional moral categories. A madam justifies her chosen profession as a way out of poverty, and argues that prostitution is a rational alternative for working-class women under capitalism. Theodore Dreiser's *Sister Carrie* (1900), written under the influence of naturalism, focuses upon the social circumstances and psychological pressures which make chastity difficult for the heroine. After having lost her job, and a berth in her older sister's household, Carrie drifts into a life as a kept woman. She is driven as much by a desire to buy pretty clothes and enjoy the nightlife of the city as by her desperate financial straits.

At the turn of the century, the works by Moore, Shaw, and Dreiser which debunked the ideal of female purity were subjected to lengthy censorship disputes. Both Mudie's and W. H. Smith, a circulating library and bookstore chain, refused to carry *Esther Waters*.[24] *Mrs. Warren's Profession*, though written in 1894, could not be performed until

1902 thanks to a ban by the Lord Chamberlain's Examiner of Plays.[25] The publisher of *Sister Carrie* required heavy emendations of the original manuscript, and even then was reluctant to publish the book.[26]

In the early years of the twentieth century, however, censorship pressures lessened, and popular fiction began to echo the representations of female sexuality found in Moore, Dreiser, and other naturalists. David Graham Phillips' *Susan Lenox: Her Fall and Rise*, completed prior to the author's death in 1911 and published in 1917, is in the vein of *Sister Carrie*. The heroine prostitutes herself in order to escape from the miseries of life in the tenements and the brutalizing effects of factory labor. As Elizabeth Janeway has pointed out in an analysis of the novel, Susan's fall is presented in Nietzschean terms, as an act of strength and self-affirmation.[27] In response to a sermon by a Salvation Army preacher, she asserts that "the wages of sin is sometimes a house on Fifth Avenue."[28] Like *Susan Lenox*, *Rain*, the 1922 play by John Colton and Clemence Randolph adapted from a short story by W. Somerset Maugham, repudiates the terms of the moral discourse directed at the fallen woman. The play focuses on a missionary worker who attempts to reform the prostitute Sadie Thompson. The missionary's treatment of Sadie is shown to be both hard-hearted—he proposes to deport her from Pago Pago to face jail in the United States—and a denial of his own sexuality. In the last act of the play, his own unconscious desire for Sadie drives him to rape and suicide. Sexuality is thus posed as an instinctual force which defies moral judgment and argument.

Although certainly not in the naturalist tradition of *Susan Lenox* or *Rain*, Anita Loos's comic best-seller *Gentlemen Prefer Blondes* (1926) takes to an extreme their cynicism about the ideal of purity. Written as a diary from the point of view of Lorelei, a kept woman, *Gentlemen Prefer Blondes* neither condemns nor justifies her sexual status. In a real departure from genre conventions, Lorelei does not even find herself in desperate circumstances; the overriding motivation for her actions is her frank and unabashed pursuit of diamonds.

The Fallen Woman Film

In the postwar period, there is a pronounced disparity between the reformers' treatment of the fallen woman genre in film and its literary counterparts. By the twenties, attempts to censor the fallen woman story in drama and popular fiction had largely abated. Of the examples cited above, censorship was attempted in only one case, that of *Susan Lenox* in 1917.[29] By the early thirties, one finds only isolated attempts to suppress fallen woman novels, such as Donald Henderson Clarke's *Female*.[30] In contrast, agitation for film censorship in this period often centered upon complaints about the "sex picture." The films became more notorious, and were eventually more closely regulated, than the literary sources from which they drew. The disparity in the treatment of film versus popular fiction derives from the ways in which censors and reformers regarded the audience for these two media. Reformers and MPPDA officials were often at pains to distinguish film from literature, and they argued that the cinema necessitated relatively stronger forms of control. In the Formula, a set of policies adopted in 1924 to govern the acquisition of literary properties by the studios, the MPPDA aimed to prevent "the prevalent type of book and play from becoming the prevalent type of picture."[31] The industry's Production Code, adopted in 1930, explained the logic of this distinction between film and literature:

> Most arts appeal to the mature. This art appeals at once to every class, mature, immature, developed, undeveloped, law abiding, criminal. Music has its grades for different classes; so has literature and drama. This art of the motion picture, combining as it does the two fundamental appeals of looking at a picture and listening to a story, at once reached [*sic*] every class of society. [Thus] it is difficult to produce films intended for only certain classes of people. . . . Films, unlike books and music, can with difficulty be confined to certain selected groups.[32]

The controversy around the fallen woman film clearly illustrates the special standards applied to the cinema as a mass medium. Versions of the story already current within the domain of popular fiction were deemed inappropriate for an audience which included children, teenage girls, and other groups defined as potentially "deviant," such as second-generation immigrants.

Much of the debate around the fallen woman genre attached to updated variants of the plot which criticized or trivialized traditional ideals of female purity. It should be noted, however, that while Hollywood was certainly influenced by contemporary literary treatments of the type, it drew material from the span of the genre's history, including nineteenth-century works from both Europe and America.[33] Adaptations from nineteenth-century sources included versions of *Anna Karenina* made in 1915, 1927 (as *Love*), and 1935; *La Dame aux camélias*, made in 1915, 1917, 1921, 1927, and 1936; and *East Lynne*, made in 1916, 1921, 1925, and 1931. In some cases even the traditional iconography of the genre was transferred to film. In *Waterloo Bridge* (1931, 1940), as in the Augustus Egg triptych described above, the bridge is the site of the fallen woman's despair and suicide. D. W. Griffith's *Way Down East* (1920), adapted from Lottie Blair Parker's popular play, contains a classic scene in which the heroine is cast out into the snow, forced to leave her domestic haven because of a past transgression. These older forms of the genre were complemented by adaptations from contemporary American literary sources. *Gentlemen Prefer Blondes* appeared in 1928. There were two versions of *Rain: Sadie Thompson* in 1928, and a second, under the original title, in 1932. MGM produced a version of *Susan Lenox: Her Fall and Rise* released in 1931, although the film softens the cynicism of the novel.

The influence of contemporary literary treatments of the genre went well beyond the specific works selected for adaptation. In a whole body of films devoted to working-class girls in an urban milieu, the stereotype of the injured innocent or world-weary demimondaine gave way to any one of a series of self-consciously "modern" American types: flappers, gold diggers, chorines, wisecracking shopgirls. While the heroine could be a kept woman, a trickster, or simply out to marry a millionaire, the stories revolved around the problem of obtaining furs, automobiles, diamonds, and clothes from men. Thus, the downward trajectory of the fall was replaced by a rise in class. Examples of this plot, dubbed the "Cinderella story" within the industry,[34] include *Manhandled* (1924), *Orchids and Ermine* (1927), *Possessed* (1931), *Bed of Roses* (1933), and *Baby Face* (1933).

The films dealing with class rise helped attract the attention of censors and reformers to the genre as a whole. While all of the variants of the fallen woman film were eventually subject to censorship by the MPPDA, the versions in which she came to a less than unhappy end made the representation of illicit sexuality especially problematic. The trajectory of the fall set the pattern for most nineteenth-century versions of the story, even given a liberal treatment of the figure of the prostitute. She was sympathetic precisely because, and to the degree that, she experienced remorse, and suffered a pronounced degradation and decline. The Hollywood films which played up the motif of class rise violated the structural underpinnings of this familiar nineteenth-century melodrama.

Like the literary works from which they drew, the films undercut the narrative logic of sin, guilt, and redemption.

There is some question about when the tendency to invert or attenuate the trajectory of the fall was initiated in Hollywood films. The vamp, a figure common in the films of the teens, often got rich at the expense of her male victims. Considered from the point of view of genre conventions, however, the vamp film seems relatively conservative. The vamp's importance lay in the dilemma which she posed for the male hero: *A Fool There Was* (1914) set up an opposition between the Theda Bara character and the hero's virtuous wife. The film turned upon the man's inability to resist the vamp's overtures, and his attendant financial and moral ruin. In contrast, films such as *Susan Lenox* or *Possessed* centered upon the difficulties of women living alone in the city; they emphasized the *heroine's* financial predicament, and her ambition and success, often in amoral terms.

Apart from the vamp film, critics have discussed the emergence of stories about class rise almost entirely with reference to the Depression. For example, according to Richard Griffith, the fallen woman cycle of the thirties addressed the wishes or fantasies of women denied material goods.[35] The aggressive heroine and the motif of class rise predate 1929, however, and in my view are better explained as a function of the transformation of melodrama in the postwar era. The earliest use of the term "gold digger" I have found is the 1919 play *The Gold Diggers*, upon which the 1923 Warner Brothers film of the same name is based. The term appears in a film of 1928, *That Certain Thing*, applied to a poor girl from the tenements who is accused of tricking a rich boy into marriage. In both *Classified* (1925) and *Manhandled* (1924), the heroine accepts clothes and other favors from a wealthy man and is tempted to become a kept woman, although she ends up married to a man of her own class. Following an oft-repeated plot formula, in *It* (1927), the heroine, a sexually aggressive flapper, pursues and finally marries her upper-class boss. The outlines of the Cinderella story are thus well codified by the mid-twenties.

The maternal melodrama, one of the largest subcategories of the fallen woman genre, raises questions of periodization akin to those of the Cinderella films. This plot concerns an errant mother who comes back into contact with her child after many years and conceals her true identity for fear of her evil past. In a lengthy discussion of the type, Christian Viviani makes a distinction between older European forms of the story and more modern, American ones.[36] He claims that the heroine's decline is less protracted in the American versions and that a happy ending, in which she is reunited with her child, more common. Viviani explains this relatively upbeat variant of the story as a New Deal parable in which the heroine is "redeemed" by work and, with her illegitimate child, comes to represent the hope of a new society. Certainly there are instances of the maternal melodrama such as La Cava's *Gallant Lady* (1933) which seem to invoke a rhetoric of unity and hope characteristic of the New Deal. But I would argue that what Viviani terms "Americanized" variants of the plot are more frequently typified by a tendency to downplay the heroine's degradation and decline in favor of upward mobility. Further, this motif predates the Depression films.

In the case of the maternal melodrama, the heroine's rise can be motivated by any one of a number of plot devices—by work or marriage. As in the Cinderella story, the alteration of the heroine's class status is marked by the acquisition of clothes, automobiles, and new living accommodations. *The Goose Woman* (1925) opens with the mother already fallen. Once a famous diva, she has become a rude and scurrilous drunkard (see Figure 1.1). A clever district attorney requires her testimony at a murder trial. In order to make her presentable in court, he has her bathed, coiffed, and elegantly dressed (see Figure 1.2). Admired and treated with dignity once again, she is able to overcome her past and is reconciled with her son.

The films of the thirties continue to highlight the beauty of the mother's clothes and new surroundings as a means of representing her reintegration into society. In *Gallant Lady,* the heroine becomes an interior decorator and tastefully redesigns the mansion of the man she eventually marries. In *Rockabye* (1932), the heroine, a woman of dubious reputation, has become wealthy as an actress. Although forced to renounce her adopted child and later her lover, she never abandons her upper-class lifestyle. She wears a succession of furs and sequined gowns throughout the film. Her house includes a formal garden and a particularly elegant black and white kitchen (see Figure 1.3). Moreover, in one sequence, she ventures back to a rowdy saloon in a poor part of the city, as various characters point out how far she has risen above her origins "in the gutter." Thus, in terms of both story and mise-en-scène, the mother's redemption is symbolized, and to a degree motivated, by the attainment of upper-class status.

The examples of the Cinderella story and the maternal melodrama give some indication of how the fallen woman plot was updated in the context of Hollywood in the twenties and early thirties. Although the

1.1 *The Goose Woman*

1.2 *The Goose Woman*

1.3 *Rockabye*

films do not entirely abandon nineteenth-century narrative and iconographic conventions, a new emphasis on social mobility, and hence
female aggressivity, overlays traditional plots and modes of characterization. Moreover, the heroine appears in increasingly lavish and exotic
settings, greatly attenuating the severity of the fall. It is as if Eve were
admitted to the Garden of Eden *after* having tasted the apple.

The Impetus for Censorship

In the thirties, the permutations of genre conventions I have described
were acknowledged, and criticized, in terms of the films' putative effects
upon real women. There was much discussion of the heroine's sexual
trespasses and in particular violations of the ideal of female chastity.
Consider a column by the film critic of the *Nation* entitled "Virtue in
1933":

> It happens that the climaxes of the two pictures seen this week, one at
> New York's largest theater and the other at one of its smallest, hinge
> on the same problem of conduct in a young girl's mind. The problem,
> of course, is not a particularly new one. Long ago there was a picture

called "Way Down East" in which Miss Lillian Gish was to be seen grappling with it. . . . The only reason that one calls attention to its recurrence as a major theme at this time is that it may serve to illustrate the profound change that has come over movie producers and audiences alike in their attitude towards this and similar problems. No longer is there a certain risk of sympathy in showing the hero in the arms of his mistress, the heroine having a child by someone other than her husband, the ingenue making a few mistakes before settling down to a closer observance of conventions.[37]

The *Nation*, a liberal magazine, takes a "moderate" view: both the industry and the public participate in a general transformation of sexual mores. But other sources, more critical of the industry, argued that this type of film affirmed and promulgated undesirable changes in sexual mores. For example, in *The Content of Motion Pictures*, one of the Payne Fund Studies, Edgar Dale noted: "Colorful and attractive stars are commonly given roles depicting women who lose their virtue, who are ruined by men, lead profligate lives."[38] Dale found this a "dangerous situation" because the use of stars in such roles made the violation of the "current moral code . . . desirable or attractive."[39] Thus, the films were criticized insofar as Hollywood was presumed to promote sex outside of marriage for women.

While commentary was directed at the representation of sexuality within the cycle, there were also complaints about the representation of money. One finds references to films which show kept women "living in luxury" or what was rather vaguely identified as "glamour." Here, for example, is a letter of complaint sent to Will Hays from Alice Ames Winter, an employee of the MPPDA

> Recent pictures from [So] *This is Africa*, through *Temple Drake*, *Baby Face*, etc. down to Constance Bennett's latest [*Bed of Roses*], which I saw the day I got back home, and which again is the story of a criminal prostitute's methods of wangling luxury out of rich men . . . the constant flow of these pictures leaves me with mental nausea. . . .[40]

An article in *Photoplay* also bemoaned the trend with an article entitled "Charm? No! No! You Must Have Glamour."[41] The main objection to this aspect of the cycle was that the films encouraged prostitution by the representation of luxury. One newspaper columnist referred to the "flourishing crop of loose ladies on the screen," suggesting that such films constituted a temptation for women in that the heroine got rich, "practical lessons in sin."[42]

The point was discussed in an academic context in one of the Payne Fund Studies already noted, Blumer and Hauser's *Movies, Delinquency and Crime.* Blumer and Hauser's analysis of delinquency extended beyond representations of violence and criminality to include what researchers described as scenes of luxury, wealth, and ease. In analyzing the film preferences of delinquent youth, Blumer and Hauser called attention to films which they claimed stimulated a desire for money, stylish clothes, goods, and cars. Here is how they explained the potential effect of the movies on adolescent girls:

> We have noted the influence of the motion pictures in instilling desires for clothes, automobiles, wealth, and ease in boys and young men and in suggesting the idea of easily attaining them. Among girls and young women this influence of the movies seems even more pronounced, for a greater premium seems to be placed on fine clothes, appearance, and a life of ease in the case of women. . . . In many cases the desire for luxury expresses itself in a smarter and more fashionable selection of clothes, house furnishings, etc., within the financial means of the girl; but, on the other hand, many of the girls and young women studied grow dissatisfied with their own clothes and manner of living and in their efforts to achieve motion picture standards frequently get into trouble.[43]

Blumer and Hauser argued further that the girl's desire for represented objects could exacerbate the process of identification with sexually delinquent female characters. The researchers also noted, without the faintest trace of irony, that the allure of Hollywood's ideal of consumption was enhanced for those from "areas of high delinquency [where] the absence of wealth is generally greatest, and the opportunities of getting it legitimately are fewest. . . ."[44]

The Payne Fund Studies thus evoked the fallen woman film in the course of an attempt to analyze the possible deleterious consequences of film viewing, especially for working-class and immigrant women. More broadly, in the popular discourse on the films, the genre served as a privileged example of the kind of sexual license that reformers objected to within the Hollywood cinema as a whole.

The Model of Self-Regulation

There is every indication that the MPPDA was aware of the nature and extent of the criticisms being directed at Hollywood. For example, writing of the film *Red Headed Woman* in 1932, an industry censor compared the figure of the gold digger and that of the gangster, and noted that in each case complaints centered upon the problem of glamour:

> There is a striking similarity between the treatment of this character and the earlier treatment of the gangster character. . . . Because he was the central figure, because he achieved power and money and a certain notoriety, our critics claimed that an inevitable attractiveness resulted. And that was what they objected to in gangster pictures. They said we killed him off but that we made him glamorous before we shot him. This is what you are apt to be charged with in this case. While the Red Headed Woman is a common little creature from over the tracks who steals other women's husbands and uses her sex attractiveness to do it, she is the central figure and it will be contended that a certain glamour surrounds her.[45]

Writing in 1933, another industry censor noted:

> [This] is undoubtably an unfortunate time to bring the kept woman on the screen again and we are doing our best to make the studio heads conscious of the fact that the piling up of sex stories at the present time may bring about a situation where it will be necessary to get the studio heads together and make an agreement to lay off this type of story such as occurred when the gangster films got too numerous.[46]

At issue, then, for the MPPDA and for the industry, was how to enact the conventions of the genre given the complaints about rich, attractive, and loose-living heroines.

But how did the presuppositions and concerns of the reform movement inflect the censorship of specific films? In what forms, and by what mechanisms, did public debate and criticism of the industry impinge upon the production process? The most extensive description of the MPPDA's policy and procedure is Raymond Moley's *The Hays Office*, published in 1945.[47] Moley, who wrote a number of books and articles on behalf of the MPPDA in the forties, had access to primary materials which until recently have not been available to researchers. As his arguments have been widely accepted, they are worth summarizing in some detail. Moley focuses on the Production Code, a statement of industry policy proposed by the MPPDA and adopted by the industry in 1930. Moley's explanation of the function of the Code adopts what may be considered a legal model of self-regulation. Like a law, the Code is thought to provide a series of prohibitions or constraints on production (with a list of topics to be avoided as well as a "Reasons" section justifying regulation as such). According to Moley, these prohibitions could not be "enforced" prior to 1934. By an agreement reached in 1930, the studios were not to release any feature that did not meet with the Studio Relations Committee's approval. When a disagreement would arise between the committee and a producer, however, an appeal would be made to a panel composed of other producers—the so-called Hollywood Jury. Since the Jury usually decided in favor of its fellow producers, the recommendations of the Studio Relations Committee were easy to ignore.

The situation changed following the events of 1933–34. The Payne Fund Studies, widely quoted and discussed in the popular press, gave rise to much negative publicity for the film industry. The Catholic Legion of Decency's widely broadcast threat of a boycott of the cinema in April of 1934 augmented this negative publicity. Moley argues that as a result of this public pressure, the MPPDA made changes in the administrative mechanisms of censorship. Hays was able to negotiate concessions from producers which made it possible to "enforce" the Code. The Studio Relations Committee was reconstituted as the Production Code Administration under Joseph Breen and the Hollywood Jury eliminated. Moley claims that as of 1934 the Production Code Administration had the power to bar a film from exhibition in any theater owned by or affiliated with any member company of the MPPDA. During this period and up until 1948, Paramount, Warners, RKO, MGM, and 20th Century-Fox, all members of the MPPDA, owned 77 percent of the important first-run theaters in the United States.[48] The Code could be enforced, then, because in the final instance a producer could not get access to the major, first-run release outlets without the approval or "seal" of the Production Code Administration.

Moley's argument hinges upon the idea that censorship had a power almost comparable to that of the legal notion of prior restraint. But it seems unlikely that the Code was simply "enforced" in the manner of a law, through the exercise of such power. This argument runs counter to evidence which has become available to us since the publication of

Moley's book in 1945: the MPPDA case files; the memoirs of a Hollywood censor, *See No Evil;* and an unpublished oral history conducted with Geoffrey Shurlock, a member of the Production Code Administration.[49] Further, considered as a model, it seems to me that the quasi-legal conception of censorship does not do justice to the peculiarities, the *specificity* of the system of self-regulation.

There is no evidence that industry censors were ever in a position routinely to block the exhibition of a film produced by one of the major studios. In direct opposition to Moley's argument, Geoffrey Shurlock, who worked under Breen in the Production Code Administration, claims that censors could not refuse to pass a film (withhold a "seal"):

> No, we never refused seals. We were in the business of granting seals. The whole purpose of our existence was to arrange pictures so that we could give seals. You had to give a seal.[50]

Shurlock's remarks make sense if one considers the economics of industry self-regulation. The MPPDA, charged with protecting the long-run interests of the industry, would hardly consider it desirable to damage profits by disturbing the regular issue of films.[51] Thus, it is not likely that withholding completed films from exhibition was adopted as a matter of standard MPPDA procedure.

I am interested not in exposing the "errors" in Moley's history but in demonstrating the difficulties inherent in explaining MPPDA policy and procedures along quasi-legal lines. The powers of and limits on self-regulation differ markedly from those of state or civil censorship bodies. It is important to distinguish between the two if we are to account for the specificity of self-regulation as a process. State censors, who were independent of the film industry, were in a position to prevent exhibition. Short of banning a film, they could alter its editing at will by excising segments from a final print. In contrast, the censors for the MPPDA exercised more power while films were in the planning stages than in the review of completed features. This description of the Production Code Administration's operating procedure by Jack Vizzard, who worked under Breen, gives a sense of the importance of preproduction:

> "Huddle" was the heart of the Code operation. . . . It started at ten o'clock sharp, like assembly call. It was nothing more or less than a story conference, in which the staff members reported on the scripts

they had read on the previous day. It was during the huddle that decisions were made and lines of strategy were drawn up as to how this problem would be met, or that riddle dealt with. After the huddle, the staff members scattered and went their separate ways, some to studios for knock-down-drag-out fights with producers, some to write letters on scripts they had covered, and some to plunge into yet another script. Keeping up with the endless flow of scripts that poured through the office was like trying to run up a hill of sand. While the main body of the work was done on the scripts before the productions reached the sound stages, the right was always reserved to see the picture also. . . .[52]

Vizzard's description of the daily meeting of the Production Code Administration as a "story conference" points to one of the basic differences between self-regulation and state censorship. Self-regulation was an integrated part of film production under the studio system. Industry censors were in a position to request revisions in scripts and, in consultation with writers, directors, and producers, to effect changes in narratives. I take this to be Shurlock's meaning when he says, "The whole purpose of our existence was to *arrange pictures* so that we could give seals" (italics mine). This is very different from a power of restraint—blocking exhibition or "cutting things out" of films. Censors participated in the decision-making process by which the studio hierarchy orchestrated and controlled production. They achieved their ends, within this hierarchy, by means of more or less successful negotiations, what Vizzard refers to as "knock-down-drag-out fights with producers."

It remains unclear, however, how the various social forces confronting the industry influenced the process of negotiation concerning specific films. If we abandon the idea that the Production Code Administration simply "enforced" the Code through the power to restrain exhibition, then it becomes necessary to propose an alternate explanation of how the social relations between the MPPDA and external groups determined censorship, especially during the tense years of 1933 and 1934. It is possible to take account of this social context if we assume that censorship sought to restructure specific films which posed some threat to the industry's political and economic interests. The process of self-regulation may then be described in terms of two distinct but related stages. The first stage—evaluation—consisted in the isolation of films or elements within films likely to offend reform groups or provoke action by government regulatory agencies. The case files indicate that the MPPDA employed a number of procedures for anticipating how external agencies might react to films. Its employees gathered information on the reception of films both domestically and abroad, and rendered expert opinions about what was likely to be found offensive. It regularly collected data on material cut by state and foreign censorship boards and reviewed letters of complaint from reform groups.

The second stage of censorship consisted in negotiations between the MPPDA and film producers. The MPPDA's object in these negotiations was to find some way of forestalling the anticipated complaints and minimizing the cuts that would be required by the state censorship boards. As a rule, however, producers did not want their films altered. They sought to retain potentially offensive genre elements which presumably had already "proven" their appeal at the box office. Thus this stage of censorship may be characterized as an attempt to compromise between the aims of the MPPDA (to eliminate potentially offensive material) and the aims of producers (to preserve this supposedly profitable material).

This account of the process of regulation does not posit a direct relationship between the demands of external agencies and the form assumed by censorship in any given case. In particular, I dispute the claim, advanced in some film histories, that after 1934 censorship reflected the values and beliefs espoused by the Catholic Legion of Decency.[53] To be sure, the MPPDA was particularly moved to respond to the Legion in this period, but, in terms of the model proposed here, regulation did not entail the simple assimilation of the demands of this or any other pressure group. In any given case the MPPDA employed devices for anticipating or projecting what would offend external agencies. Theoretically it could be, and in fact it sometimes was, wrong in this anticipation. Even after 1934 the MPPDA released films which offended the Catholic Legion of Decency and were given a "Condemned" rating.[54] Further, even if the MPPDA correctly anticipated the demands of external agencies, censorship proper consisted in a series of compromises between it and producers. The utopian ideal of self-regulation was to forestall criticism while at the same time allowing the producer maximal use of his original material. In practice there was continual tension, a kind of push-pull, between conflicting aims or tendencies. Thus censorship as an institutional process did not simply reflect social pressures; it articulated a strategic response to them. And this strategy was worked out on a case-by-case basis, before films went into production.

The usefulness of strategy as a concept for analyzing censorship is that it explains the logic of determination in terms of a dynamic interplay of aims and interests, rather than a cause—the Catholic Legion of Decency—which unilaterally produces an effect—the enforcement of the Code. The model allows for, indeed leads us to expect, a certain variation from film to film, since there would be some latitude in defining problems and arriving at compromises. Yet this model can also account for broader changes in the administration of censorship following the publication of the Payne Fund Studies and the Catholic Legion of Decency campaign.

Consider a problem which censors identified relatively frequently: "adultery is made attractive." As a matter of routine, sometimes with reference to previous cases in which adultery had been a question, censors and producers would work out a compromise which permitted some representation of this act. Certain compromises would thus become institutionalized, repeated, with slight variation, from film to film. These routines were altered following the events of 1934. In the face of escalating public criticism of the industry, censors were in a position to negotiate relatively more extensive revisions of films and scripts. Breen was particularly careful to refine the definition of what was acceptable under the Code. So producers needed to devise and employ a new set of representational strategies in order to justify or defend what censors deemed potentially offensive. There was a more far-reaching transformation, a different narrative elaboration, of offensive material.

This study thus posits censorship as a constructive force, in the sense that it helped to shape film form and narrative.[55] Making comparisons between the MPPDA's treatment of films before and after 1934, it seeks to ascertain differences in the representation of illicit sexuality, money, and class rise in these two periods. It is my contention that the rules censors developed for the treatment of the fallen woman film were primarily concerned with the *structures* of narrative—the nature of endings, motivation of action, patterns of narration. I seek to describe the development of these narrative strategies of censorship and to delineate their implications for Hollywood's representations of female sexuality and its construction of sexual difference.

Before 1934, negotiations between producers and industry censors involved discrete and localized elements of the text. Shots or lines of dialogue which censors deemed offensive might be eliminated or transformed. Frequently, a scene would be added in which the fallen woman's actions were denounced, or emphasis would be placed on her (the film's) unhappy end. After 1934, censors were able to negotiate relatively more systematic alterations of narrative. When evaluating scripts, censors routinely suggested alterations in plot—in the way in which the films motivated the fall and in the consequences which could follow from sexual transgression. A number of narrative strategies could delay or redirect the trajectory of class rise. Often the films stressed the heroine's abasement or punishment rather than her acquisition of wealth. In some cases, the films used some form of narration such as voice-over, opening titles, or a character telling a story in flashback, all of which more or less ambiguously proposed criticisms of the fallen woman's sexual transgressions and her aspirations to wealth.

Self-regulation was not, however, a smooth or completely successful operation. The public response to the fallen woman film, as well as the many disputes between the MPPDA and film producers, suggest that in many cases the MPPDA did not succeed in its efforts to alleviate causes for complaint. One must then explain not only how censorship affected narrative, but also the gaps or inconsistencies in its routines.

This question touches on an area of debate concerning what has been called the subversive or progressive text. Seeking to theorize the relationship between the classical Hollywood text and ideology, a number of critics, most prominently the collective associated with the *Cahiers du Cinéma* in the seventies, have proposed that certain films depart from the transparency and narrative closure typical of the classical text, thereby revealing the ideological presuppositions which underlie it.[56] Feminist critics such as Claire Johnston have been interested in the idea of such "readings against the grain" and have sought to identify mainstream Hollywood films which critique the dominant cinema from within the terms of its mode of address.[57] It is tempting to argue that at least certain examples of the fallen woman cycle constitute subversive texts in Johnston's sense of the term. This is to suggest not that the films directly set out to challenge the values of marriage, hard work, and female chastity, but rather that in their terms of address and enactment of narrative conventions the films inadvertently destabilize the moral and sexual categories which censorship sought to reinforce.

The very notion of a subversive text must be approached with caution, however. This mode of analysis has been criticized as anachronistic and historically untenable. For example, Richard Maltby argues that the process of finding subversive meanings is unbounded, "restrained only by the subjectivity of the critic," and thus necessarily ahistorical.[58] The problem is the status of textual analysis as evidence, that is, finding viable ways to delimit and contextualize the process of interpretation.

Because industry self-regulation functioned as a sort of machine for registering and internalizing social conflict, it provides an extraordinarily fruitful means of contextualizing film analysis. In the case studies presented here, I have sought to examine films through the grid of the MPPDA's concerns. Archival materials such as production and story files and the case files of the MPPDA have served as a basis for identifying what was considered offensive, morally repugnant, or politically dangerous.

I have chosen six representative cases for analysis out of an initial sample of one hundred titles. The sample includes films made between 1929, when the MPPDA first began to monitor scripts on the West Coast on a regular basis, and 1942, when the system of self-regulation becomes complicated by the Office of War Information's attempt to monitor scripts through its Bureau of Motion Pictures.[59] (See Appendix: Censorship Cases Reviewed for further discussion of the composition of the sample.) There were two criteria for selecting a film for close analysis. First, that film had to have occasioned a statement of MPPDA policy. In some cases, the files contain correspondence between industry censors and Will Hays concerning how a particular type of problem was to be handled. Such instances are instructive because they permit some generalizations about MPPDA routine. A second criterion for selecting a case was that it had to indicate some of the social constraints which had an impact on the formulation of policy. The data compiled by the MPPDA show that some films were heavily censored by external agencies. In several cases, films were banned outright by the New York state board and had to be reedited before their release. Other files contain letters of complaint or clippings of newspaper articles which report low or "condemned" ratings by the Catholic Legion of Decency. Thus, I have been able to single out films which we know in fact went beyond the bounds of the acceptable. These lapses or failures of self-regulation are important for they illuminate the social forces which motivated censorship. In a very real sense, such limit cases defined what was not permissible within the range of films which composed the cycle.

I have used the MPPDA case files not only as a basis for the selection of films, but also as a guide in the process of analysis. The files contain letters and memos in which censors discuss their objections to a script and provide suggestions for revisions. These documents call attention to specific moments of difficulty or stress. Further, by correlating the MPPDA correspondence, the successive drafts of the screenplay, and the completed film, I have charted how material deemed unacceptable came to be represented. Thus as a methodological principle, all of the extant written materials—drafts of screenplays, memos in which censors rewrote scenes or proposed readings of scripts—are placed at the same level of importance as the film itself. The object of study is, in effect, expanded to include not only the film as such but the entire process of revision. The analysis is concerned with the strategic logic which underlies this process: for example, it seeks to determine if the completed film emphasizes moral questions in a different way than the first draft of the screenplay, or if the events of the plot have been reordered to eliminate a potentially offensive scene from the completed feature.

This approach provides a sense of the *mechanisms* by which social conflicts impinged on a given text—that is, through the protracted negotiations and disputes between the MPPDA and the studios. Further, through sources such as the MPPDA case files it becomes possible to document, with some precision, the *way these conflicts surfaced in representation*—that is, as choices among various versions of the script. Analyzing the differences between these versions permits us to reconstruct the complex network of explicit rules and implicit narrative constraints which determined what was deemed aberrant or acceptable. Further, textual analysis, particularly a discussion of film style, suggests some of the ways these constraints could be circumvented or displaced. Finally, by comparing films across the decade, one can begin to get a sense of how the constraints imposed on representation changed over time. Thus, it becomes possible to delineate what was deviant or unusual within the films of the early thirties in relation to a clearly specified norm—the later versions of the cycle which were approved by the MPPDA.

2

The Studio Relations Committee's
Policies and Procedures

THE STUDIO RELATIONS COMMITTEE was the division of the MPPDA responsible for the administration of censorship. It is usually said to have been an ineffectual organization, unable to enforce the terms of the Production Code until its reconstitution as the Production Code Administration in 1934. However, an examination of the MPPDA case files reveals that the office was in fact active in the period 1929–34. It employed five, possibly six, men and its director, Jason Joy, was frequently successful in negotiating with producers. Indeed, in this period, censors formulated objections to the fallen woman film and devised basic strategies for dealing with the genre which continued to operate, albeit in more elaborated forms, even after 1934. To argue, then, that it was relatively easier for films to bypass the constraints of censorship in this period is not to suggest that there were no constraints at all.

A discussion of the overall aims and structure of the MPPDA will provide a context for understanding the organizational hierarchy responsible for the administration of self-regulation in the early thirties. From the time of its formation in 1922, the MPPDA, under the leadership of Will Hays, performed many functions aside from censorship. Partly in response to the star scandals of the early twenties, Hays set up an active public relations department that monitored both press coverage of Hollywood and the complaints about the industry voiced by women's, civic, and church organizations.[1] In this same period, Hays established the MPPDA's office of foreign relations and consistently lobbied European governments to prevent the imposition of tariffs or import quotas that would have been detrimental to the industry's foreign markets.[2] Hays also developed several programs which aimed at regularizing trade practices in the sphere of distribution and exhibition. The association helped the studios to formulate a standard film exhibition contract and created film boards of trade to arbitrate disputes between distributor and exhibitor.[3] In his discussion of antitrust litigation in the twenties, Michael Conant suggests that these boards of trade served as a means of enforcing blockbooking agreements and also constituted a forum in which the five largest distributors divided up the exhibition market and entered price-fixing agreements.[4] The association intervened in the sphere of production, as well as distribution, on behalf of the major studios. Letters from Fred Beetson and Pat Riley to Hays indicate that the MPPDA helped to coordinate the action taken by the studios against the craft unions that were forming in the twenties and early thirties.[5] Clearly, the MPPDA served to orchestrate unilateral action among previously competing firms, offering its members opportunities for increased profits and the mutual protection of their interests.

The MPPDA maintained a limited form of censorship from its New York offices after 1924. As I have noted, the association examined popular books and plays slated for acquisition by the studios under the terms of an agreement known as the Formula. One of Hays's assistants, Maurice McKenzie, administered the process of rewriting and retitling literary properties considered potentially offensive.[6] In 1927 the MPPDA also devised the "Don'ts and Be Carefuls," a list for film producers of topics likely to provoke reform groups or state censor boards.[7] But there were no institutional mechanisms for the application of the "Don'ts and Be Carefuls"; that is, the association did not regularly review original screenplays or completed features in this period.

Censorship on the West Coast began in 1928 when Jason Joy was dispatched from New York and, among his other duties, established an office for the purpose of monitoring scripts before they went into production.[8] In 1930, the MPPDA's member companies formally adopted the Production Code as a set of guidelines for self-regulation and agreed to submit their scripts to Joy's office. While in 1930 some producers apparently tried to slip projects into production without giving industry censors the opportunity of review, by 1931 Joy described submission as "mandatory" and it seems to have become a routine part of preproduction.[9]

Throughout the early thirties, West Coast censors frequently consulted with their superiors in the east. The head of the Studio Relations Committee reported to Hays and sometimes to Maurice McKenzie. He made a weekly report concerning all the scripts under review and contacted Hays by telegram or telephone to discuss specific cases. As a rule, Hays did not intervene in the day-to-day activities of the Studio

Relations Committee, although on occasion he viewed completed films and also mediated disputes between the Studio Relations Committee and producers.

A letter to Hays of October 1932 suggests a division of labor between the director of the Studio Relations Committee—who established policy and was responsible for various negotiations—and the other members of his staff, each of whom read scripts, following a given number of stories through production (see Figure 2.1).[10] During the early thirties, there were several important changes in personnel in which employees moved from the New York offices of the MPPDA to Hollywood. Jason Joy, who had worked in New York in the twenties, moved to the West Coast in 1928.[11] I have not found a complete list of his staff but the movements of some individuals can be deduced from letters and case files. Lamar Trotti moved to Los Angeles from the New York office sometime before December 15, 1931.[12] He appears to have been fairly highly placed in the

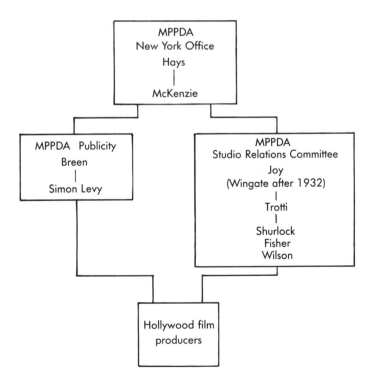

2.1 Reporting Structure of Industry Censors

office hierarchy since he negotiates with Irving Thalberg of MGM in Joy's absence in the case of *Red Headed Woman*.[13] A letter to Hays of 1933 mentions two more employees involved in "studio work" (possibly reading scripts): Mr. (Geoffrey) Shurlock and Mr. Fisher.[14]

In 1932, Joy left the MPPDA to become an executive at Fox, and was followed there by Lamar Trotti, who took a position as screenwriter. James Wingate, head of the New York state censor board, was appointed director of the Studio Relations Committee in September 1932, a post he held until December 1933.[15] Despite his connection with Fox, however, Joy maintained contact with Hays and seems to have exercised administrative control of the office during the opening months of Wingate's tenure. Joy writes Hays in October indicating that he is still in a position of power:

> It occurs to me that it would be wise, for the time being, to retain as much of the practice and personnel of the present office as possible until Dr. Wingate is thoroughly familiar with all that is going on, at which time I would expect him to make recommendations to you which you might put into effect more or less permanently. . . . Meantime, I have been experimenting in the use of him as sort of an administrative officer.[16]

Hays's papers also contain a series of letters from Joy in April and May 1933 concerning difficulties in the administration of censorship.

During Wingate's brief tenure, Joseph Breen, who assumed control of the Production Code Administration after 1934, also participated in the administration of the Studio Relations Committee. While I have not had access to enough case files to be able to estimate the number of films reviewed by Breen in 1932 and 1933, some examples indicate that he was employed in an important advisory capacity. He carried out the evaluation of the first script of *Ann Vickers* (RKO).[17] In the case of *A Man's Castle* (Columbia), the New York office asked Breen to negotiate after Wingate became locked in a dispute with the studio management.[18] He was also involved in negotiations concerning *The Story of Temple Drake* and *Baby Face*.[19]

Thus control of the Studio Relations Committee was relatively diffused, divided between New York and Hollywood and split even further among individuals on the West Coast. Will Hays was well informed about the activities of the office and occasionally participated in the evaluation of films and scripts. After 1932, James Wingate was nominally in charge of the Studio Relations Committee although he shared control with Jason Joy. Breen acted as a consultant to Wingate, administered his own office and, in both capacities, engaged in negotiations with producers.

In discussing the MPPDA's routine for revising films, I should stress the immediate, and pragmatic, interests self-regulation served. Self-regulation was a function of the interplay between the film industry and a loose coalition of reform groups and state regulatory agencies. The MPPDA was poised between the film industry and the various external agencies which comprised its "enemies." For the early thirties, it is difficult to provide a summary of the specific threats which confronted the industry. These forces were not centralized and included many civic and church organizations in shifting patterns of alliance. Garth Jowett has shown that from the mid-twenties, a coalition of women's and Protestant groups sought government regulation of the industry.[20] A typical example, and one of the most active advocates of federal control of the movies, was the Federal Motion Picture Council.[21] An alliance of Presbyterian ministers and members of the Women's Christian Temperance Union, this group objected to films on moral grounds and sought reform through the creation of a federal censorship board. In addition, along with other reform groups, they advocated the elimination of the industry marketing strategy of blockbooking, arguing that exhibitors were forced to show immoral films. A number of religious journals, especially the nondenominational *Christian Century,* also proposed these measures. Toward their ends, the proponents of reform supported legislation in Congress, most prominently the Upshaw Bill of 1926, but also the Brookhart Bill of 1929 and the Hudson Bill of 1930.[22]

While the industry faced opposition from groups which posed the *threat* of government regulation, it also had to contend with existing government regulatory agencies. In 1933, *The Film Daily Yearbook* listed state censorship boards in Florida, New York, Massachusetts, Kansas, Ohio, Pennsylvania, Virginia, and Maryland. The boards' sphere of influence actually extended beyond these states, as Ira Carmen explains:

> The movie industry divides the nation into multi-state geographical areas for purposes of distribution so that each of these sectors is serviced by one exchange center. If deletions are ordered by a state censorship board, the distributor . . . will simply alter the particular

movie as ordered and send it along to the exhibitors within the total exchange area in its expurgated condition. Thus, before the demise of the Ohio law, West Virginia and Kentucky saw movies that had been censored in Ohio while Massachusetts' requirement carried over into Rhode Island, Vermont and New Hampshire.[23]

These boards posed various problems for film distribution and exhibition. Since producers paid a fee based upon the footage reviewed, submission to the boards represented a form of taxation. The boards sometimes banned films, and more frequently they would excise portions of prints. Such excisions created gaps in the narrative line, upset the "matching" between shots and, in the early period of sound technology, disturbed the synchronization of sound and image.

In my view, the state censor boards comprised the single most important external factor confronting the MPPDA in the early thirties. The Studio Relations Committee directed most of its activity toward avoiding state interference in exhibition and distribution. Several kinds of data support this claim. In comparison with the late thirties, there is a great deal more correspondence with the members of the boards in this period, in an effort both to get films passed and to learn of local censorship requirements. In one letter, Hays states that the head of the Studio Relations Committee is supposed to be an expert on the boards, able to anticipate their responses. Further, his decision, in 1932, to hire the head of the New York state censor board in an important position within the Studio Relations Committee can be seen as an attempt to acquire expertise in dealing with state censors.[24]

It seems clear that in its interactions with the boards, the MPPDA frequently acted in the immediate interests of the major film producers, helping to anticipate and bypass difficulties with state censors. This is an important point for it is often assumed that the MPPDA advocated moral reform against, and in spite of, the industry. But the MPPDA was able to enact industry-wide policies of censorship precisely because these benefited the film production companies, serving as a means of defense against external interference in distribution and exhibition.

While the MPPDA acted on behalf of its member companies, it must be noted that studio personnel resisted its efforts to regulate production. The MPPDA case files are a record of internecine squabbles; producers and directors engaged in prolonged and often heated debates with industry censors and, as I have noted, in the early thirties sometimes put films into production without giving the MPPDA the opportunity of review. A distinction between the short-run self-interests of production firms and the long-run collective interests of the industry helps to explain the conflict between individual producers and their trade association. Individual producers were more likely to be motivated by short-run interests—the maximization of box office receipts for single films—and on these grounds were willing to take the risk of state interference, at least in certain cases. In contrast, the MPPDA had concerns which went well beyond box office receipts for a given feature. Industry censors sought to preserve good long-term relations with the state censor boards, as well as to prevent the release of films likely to provoke drastic action by reform groups or bring on the passage of further regulatory legislation. There were grounds for conflict, then, insofar as individual firms did not need to respond to the threats which confronted the industry as a whole over time. Geoffrey Shurlock, who worked as an MPPDA censor, sums up this situation quite succinctly:

> The man who makes a film wants to find out if anybody is going to see it. That's his first consideration: will anybody go? And my consideration: is anybody complaining about it? That's our problem but not his. His problem is to get them in there.[25]

Indeed, there could be direct conflict between the aims of the MPPDA and those of production firms in cases where the MPPDA interfered with the use of what producers deemed exploitable material.

Strategies for dealing with the fallen woman cycle evolved through the process of anticipating the reactions of the boards and negotiating revisions with producers. Via confrontations with the state boards and reform groups, the Studio Relations Committee came to recognize the "sex picture" as a type which posed difficulties. And it seems fairly clear that the genre was discussed similarly outside the industry—by members of the boards, in popular and academic sources—and by industry censors. All of these sources employ the terms "glamour" and "luxury" in discussing films in which the fallen woman becomes rich, and there is general agreement that the films undermine accepted moral/sexual norms through the heroine's rise to wealth. The Studio Relations Committee also replicates the external agencies in its concern with what were considered attacks on the ideal of female chastity and fidelity in marriage. But while the Studio Relations Committee was cognizant of the complaints which issued from the public sphere, its primary function was not to prevent the production of films within the cycle, but rather to protect and perpetuate it in the face of external obstacles. That is, the process of revision did not eliminate the emphasis upon class rise or the heroine's sexual transgressions. Rather, it consisted in a series of compromises which permitted this material to survive in some form. These defensive maneuvers were highly routinized, indeed sometimes spelled out as a matter of industry policy.

The industry's Production Code was put to distinct uses within the context of the MPPDA's attempt to deal with reform groups and state censors. The industry faced a largely decentralized conglomeration of external groups each with its own program and unique set of concerns. In its formulations of industry policy, the MPPDA itself produced some consensus among these diverse entities. The Code may be regarded as a summation, a codification, of topics most frequently found to be objectionable. According to Raymond Moley, the "Reasons" section of the Code, the general statement of policy, was written by the Catholics Martin Quigley and Father Daniel Lord, but the list of topics to avoid was written at the request of Hays and reflected the MPPDA's experiences with the boards.[26] Geoffrey Shurlock explains how the state censor boards influenced the compilation of this list of topics:

> SHURLOCK: . . . Most of these items—I will make a quick educated guess—were based on the practical experience Joy had with the censor boards. That was one of the things he had to do when he was the studio relations committee. If there was trouble in Pennsylvania with an MGM picture, he was expected to go there, perhaps with somebody from the New York office, and try to get the picture out of hock. And the items that he found that were most commonly objected to, and were deleted—
> WALL: So in a way the Code was really first written by the censor boards throughout the country?
> SHURLOCK: That's why we have a Code. Because we have censor boards.
> WALL: To meet their concerns.
> SHURLOCK: Head them off at the pass.[27]

Moreover, following its adoption in 1930, both state censors and reform groups began to frame their complaints and criticisms in terms of whether or not films violated the Code. Thus it constituted at least a general consensus among the industry's critics and served censors as a guide to what would be seen as offensive.

Aside from its diagnostic function, the Code served as a basis for discussion and debate between state censors, industry censors, and producers. As a statement of policy it provided some rudimentary guidelines for the representation of problematic material. Consider the entry on adultery: "Adultery and illicit sex, sometimes necessary plot material, must not be explicitly treated or justified, or presented attractively." The language of the Code suggests the issues to be negotiated: the explicitness of the representation (what can be directly shown as opposed to what can be suggested) and the way in which the act is motivated and commented upon within the narrative (it must not be "justified" or made "attractive"). The language of the Code does not always make provisions of this kind. For example, one entry baldly states that "sex perversion or any inference to [sic] it is forbidden." However, the entries on crime and violence, adultery, and what are called "scenes of passion" and seduction give leeway for discussion as to how this material should be and could be used. Thus, within the process of self-regulation, the Code did not operate as a set of hard-and-fast rules but rather facilitated the task of anticipating public reaction to a film and established guidelines within which producers and industry censors would discuss specific problems.

In dealing with the fallen woman cycle, and probably other kinds of film as well, the MPPDA used two basic strategies of censorship. The first concerned what were sometimes called "censor worries," material considered directly vulnerable to cuts by state censors. The second concerned characterization and the broad outlines of the plot (as opposed to specific scenes likely to be cut by the boards). Both strategies aimed at reducing the number of deletions required by the boards, in the first case by altering the representation of a particularly offensive idea or action so as to get it through without cuts, and in the second by altering the outline of the plot as a whole so as to justify or defend the inclusion of potentially offensive material.

The negotiations concerning specific ideas or actions were generally resolved through the use of indirect modes of representation. Ideally, for the Studio Relations Committee, it would be impossible to pinpoint the moment of the heroine's transgressions, or to say with any certainty how, or even if, they occurred. In this imaginary example, offensive ideas could survive, but at the price of an instability of meaning. In practice, however, the Studio Relations Committee met with resistance from the studios, which sought to reduce ambiguity wherever possible. Thus, there was constant negotiation about how explicit films could be and by what means (through the image, sound, language) they could represent offensive ideas.

The process of negotiation is particularly evident at two levels: in the treatment of dialogue, and in the construction of blatantly offensive scenes or sequences. Words such as "prostitute" and "kept woman" were routinely eliminated, not only because the expressions were considered offensive in themselves but also because they marked the heroine's status too bluntly. While it was possible to make a film about a kept woman, it was not considered advisable to call attention to this in dialogue. Thus, relatively more oblique means of indicating her status became a point of negotiation and eventual compromise. For example, in the case of *The Easiest Way*, the studio asked the Studio Relations Committee if the phrase "immoral woman" was acceptable. More frequently, problems of language were bypassed entirely. Music or visuals, which were not as closely scrutinized by either the Studio Relations Committee or the boards, were used to suggest what could not be explicitly stated. For example, in numerous films of the period, among them *Baby Face, Blonde Venus*, and *Female*, the image of the heroine on the streets is used to imply the possibility of prostitution (see Figures 2.2–2.6).

In contrast with problems of language, the negotiations concerning specific scenes revolved around the visual depiction of material defined as offensive. Most obviously, the sex act could not be shown along with a number of related actions—seductions, and frequently, money changing hands. In such cases the studio would generally resort to a rather calculated use of ellipsis. Paramount's *The Story of Temple Drake*, an adaptation of William Faulkner's *Sanctuary*, provides a particularly neat example. The novel describes a rape in which the impotent Popeye employs a corn cob. Censors would have preferred that this incident be written out of the screenplay entirely, but the studio found a way to retain at least a portion of the original plot. A plot device is contrived so that, at the moment of the rape, the lights suddenly go out. While the spectator's vision is blocked, a woman's scream is heard. The film then cuts to another scene. The ellipsis clearly serves to circumvent cuts by the boards—the rape has already been removed, in the sense that it is not made visually explicit. While the Studio Relations Committee agreed upon this method of filming the rape, negotiations between industry censors and producers concerned how far the film could approach

2.2 *Baby Face*. Lily and a companion, new to the city, flirt with a cop to obtain information.

2.3 *Baby Face*

2.4 *Blonde Venus.* Helen picks up a detective who has been following her.

2.5 *Blonde Venus*

2.6 *Blonde Venus*

Faulkner's version, even by suggestion; specifically, if it was possible to include a shot of a corn cob before the black out.[28] This example indicates, then, something of the continual interplay between industry censors who strove to eliminate certain offensive ideas through ellipsis, and the studio which generally strove to find some way of suggesting what could not be directly filmed. This dynamic could give rise to quite complex uses of rhetoric, as films employed various indirect means of figuring the elided action.

In the course of negotiations with the studios, then, the Studio Relations Committee adopted a relatively coherent stance—a preference for indirect modes of representation—which was more or less enforced in the treatment of dialogue and individual scenes. This attention to specific details was seconded by more general discussion of story and character, in which industry censors sought to render a film as a whole acceptable to the boards. In this regard censors displayed a marked preference for a kind of moral didacticism. Their negotiating stance was justified with reference to the Production Code, in particular the section entitled "Reasons Supporting Preamble" which discusses the film spectator. The Code states:

> It has often been argued that art in itself is unmoral, neither good nor bad. This is perhaps true of the THING which is music, painting, poetry etc. But the thing is the PRODUCT of some person's mind, and the intention of that mind was either good or bad morally when it produced the thing. Besides, the thing has its EFFECT upon those who come into contact with it. In both these ways, that is, as a product of a mind and as the cause of definite effects, it has a deep moral significance and an unmistakable moral quality. Hence: The motion pictures, which are the most popular of modern arts for the masses, have their moral quality from the intention of the minds which produced them and from their effects on the moral lives and reactions of their audiences.[29]

Since films affect the morals of audiences, it is argued that they must safeguard moral standards. The Code directs that "the sympathy of the audience shall never be thrown to the side of crime, wrong-doing, evil or sin." In line with this statement of policy, the Studio Relations Committee often evaluated scripts in terms of the audience's engagement with and perceptions of character. And it advocated that the studios pass moral judgments on characters for the benefit of the audience. The single most important means of doing this was some form of final retribution. The Studio Relations Committee always discussed the ending of the script and advised producers against happy endings where "evil" would be rewarded. It also encouraged the studios to include what I call denunciation scenes, in which the heroine was chastized or reproached, and, in some cases, to specify other characters as "good." These sorts of revisions were referred to under the so-called "rule of compensating moral values."

Alongside explicit formulas, such as the rule of compensating moral values, censorship also relied on certain implicit narrative conventions. While these were not identified or named as such, they formed the backdrop for the ways in which censors interpreted scripts and the kinds of revisions they requested in plots. Most obviously, genre convention played a role in the Studio Relations Committee's routine treatment of the fallen woman cycle. Censorship can be seen as an attempt to reinstate nineteenth-century variants of the fall, in which the heroine's suffering and remorse were heightened, and the story often culminated in a moment of sublime self-sacrifice. As a matter of routine, industry censors frequently suggested that the element of self-sacrifice or regret be emphasized in scripts in which they foresaw difficulties. An archetypical example of the kind of narrative apotheosis approved by industry censors is Marguerite Gautier's renunciation of her lover for his own good in *La Dame aux camélias*. Scenes of this type were considered instances of the rule of compensating moral values.

The importance traditionally accorded to romantic courtship within the classical Hollywood cinema, while not a convention directly acknowledged by industry censors as such, was also of primary strategic value. At both a narrative and a symbolic level, the classical text resolves conflict through what Raymond Bellour calls the formation of the couple.[30] The disharmony or disruption which initiates the story is resolved "happily" insofar as the woman assumes a position within the couple as loyal wife or sweetheart. Censorship improvised upon the convention of the happy end according to a logic of compensation. Emphasis upon the heroine's final domestication was used to negate or counteract her sexual transgressions. In practice, the process of compensation took various forms. Given the heroine's adultery or exploitation of men, the Studio Relations Committee usually called for her punishment. In the most extreme cases, they requested that she be left destitute and alone, as in many nineteenth-century variants of the plot. Such an ending centers upon the couple, but in a negative sense: the heroine's failure to assume the position of wife and/or mother is the measure of her punishment. The studios usually preferred a more modern, that is to say relatively less punitive, version of the ending. The heroine would be "reformed" through some subterfuge such as the gold digger's conversion to "true love," a device which would permit the reconciliation of the couple. In most cases, a compromise was reached in which the heroine underwent some kind of punishment prior to the final moment of reconciliation. For example, in both *Baby Face* and *Blonde Venus*, the heroine's return to her husband is predicated upon the loss of her fortune (an inversion of her "rise"). In all of these cases, the terms of resolution have a strategic value; they affirm the familial norm and in so doing soften or attenuate the heroine's deviance, the material deemed potentially offensive.

Censors did not invent, nor did they induce producers to invent, radically new plots. Self-regulation seized upon highly familiar narrative devices, seeking to bring out moral values and judgments which were, to a large extent, already implicit in the given body of nineteenth-century genre conventions. But, while censorship did not necessarily instill new permutations of the fallen woman story, it is important to recognize that it did assign a very precise function to these conventions within a given institutional context: the rules about endings, the emphasis upon the heroine's punishment and self-condemnation all served to mitigate the possibility of cuts from the state boards and as a hedge against complaints from reform groups.

The Easiest Way

I have not been able to locate a print of MGM's *The Easiest Way*.[31] But even though the film is not available, some scripts and other production materials survive and there are pressing reasons for considering them here. *The Easiest Way* is clearly a limit case, described by MGM's Canadian distributor as "the most difficult picture as regards [government] censorship that we have ever distributed in this country."[32] It is also one of the earliest applications of the Code to the fallen woman cycle (the Code was adopted in February and preproduction on *The Easiest Way* began in October of 1930). As such it was the occasion of negotiations between Joy and producers, and more unusually, between Joy and James Wingate, then head of the New York state censor board, concerning what was acceptable under the terms of the new policy. In the course of their negotiations, Joy and Wingate articulate their respective positions on endings and the censorship of "details"—specific actions and lines of dialogue. In particular, the case demonstrates how the emphasis upon endings could serve as a defensive maneuver, permitting the representation of "details" or material otherwise likely to be cut by the boards.

The film *The Easiest Way* was an adaptation of a popular stage play produced by David Belasco in 1909 which had itself generated a good deal of controversy in the prewar period.[33] Although the story concerns the heroine's rise in class, it is not entirely typical of the thirties since the heroine is not a gold digger, that is, she does not actively pursue men for their money. Laura Murdock comes from a large and poor immigrant family living in a New York City tenement. When she obtains a job as a model in an ad agency, she is seduced by the boss, Brockton, who provides her with furs, an automobile, and pearls. Upon visiting her married sister, Peg, she is banned from the house, and by implication cut off from her family, by her brother-in-law, Nick. Traveling out west with Brockton, she meets John Madison, another character with an unsavory past, a newspaperman on leave because of a drinking problem. They fall in love and he takes an assignment in Central America to earn money so they can be married. She agrees to wait for him in New York and support herself. But in New York Laura finds it impossible to obtain another job as a model. A series of difficulties follow. She does not receive any word from Madison. Living in a cheap hotel room, she earns barely enough to send money to her sick mother. When her mother dies, she remains ostracized from her family at the funeral. In desperate circumstances and unable to pay the rent, she goes back to living with Brockton, promising him that she will write to Madison and break off their engagement. Her failure to do this precipitates a climactic scene upon Madison's return, when both men become enraged at what they consider her betrayal. The first complete draft of the screenplay sketches out two possible endings.[34] In one, Laura, abandoned by both men, goes off to a nightclub to pick up another "meal ticket." The final image is of her on the stairs, dressed in ermine, having become, in the words of the script, the incarnation of the flapper. The second ending, called the "protection" ending in the script, takes place some years after Laura has been abandoned. In a rather seedy speakeasy she meets Madison, who has reverted to drink. The two are reconciled.

As far as I have been able to determine, the sequence of negotiations on this script ran as follows. Joy reviewed the first complete draft in a letter of November 10, 1930, and was dissatisfied with both proposed endings. A memo refers to a meeting between Joy and Hunt Stromberg, the producer in charge of this particular project.[35] (Although most of the correspondence is addressed to Irving Thalberg, as head of production, most of the actual negotiations seem to have taken place with Stromberg.) At this meeting, a new ending was suggested along with revision of dialogue and other details of action. The film must have gone into production by mid-November, but a number of scenes, including new versions of the ending, were written in late November and early December.[36] On December 18, Joy writes of having seen the film at a preview the night before and requests further alterations.[37] Apparently MGM did some retakes and shot an ending which is given in the cutting continuity script of December 31, 1930.[38] I assume this reflects MGM's final version of the film.

The original script contained a number of elements which Joy considered directly vulnerable to state censorship.[39] A major point of contention with the studio was dialogue and action that explicitly marked the relationship between Laura and Brockton. Thus, Joy recommended cutting out the words "kept woman" addressed to the heroine. He also warned against the action of Brockton kissing Laura on the neck (which was described in the script). It is likely that this kind of bodily contact, in and of itself, was considered offensive, but also the action called attention to the sexual aspect of the liaison, that is, it emphasized what censors sought to leave implicit or indirect.

Joy also called for the ambiguous treatment of scenes which showed Laura and Brockton sharing an apartment. He asked the producer to invent ways to play these scenes so as to leave open the possibility that the couple were not livng together, e.g., Joy advised that Brockton appear fully dressed at breakfast time, as if he had stopped in to "visit." While other films discussed here, most notably *Blonde Venus*, utilize ambiguity as a strategy for getting potentially offensive material past the boards, MGM did not comply in this case. This was probably because the plot dictated against the use of ambiguity, particularly at the moment of the film's climax. When Madison returns from South America, Laura cannot bring herself to confess that she has renewed her arrangement with Brockton. Brockton precipitates the final confrontation between these two. He returns home from work unexpectedly, opens the door with his own key, requests his smoking jacket and by other means reveals that he and Laura have been living together. The unambiguous avowal of the relationship is therefore vital to the melodrama in that it motivates Madison's reaction to Laura's betrayal.

Another difficulty posed by the liaison between Laura and Brockton was the representation of money. An early version of the script makes it clear, in dialogue, that the attraction of Brockton for Laura is his money. Here, for example, is an excerpt from the seduction scene in the first complete draft of the script:

> Look here Laura, let me put you into a home that's fit for you (putting his arm around her). What do you think soft colors and beautiful furnishings are made for? A beauty like yours ought to have a background—a lovely setting with soft lights and luxurious surroundings. It's all waiting for you, dear. (He has drawn her up to him). Will you come to it? FADE OUT. [40]

In later versions of the script this dialogue has been eliminated, Brockton simply offers to "help" Laura, and take care of her family. [41] However, all of the versions of the script provide for the representation of luxury at the visual level. There are lengthy descriptions of Brockton's office (described as "rich" and "futuristic") and his apartment. Further,

Laura's acquiescence to Brockton's proposition is signaled through a series of short scenes in which she acquires objects—a car, a sable coat, and pearls. The screenwriter included a note which emphasizes the importance of visual display in these scenes:

> The intention of the above vignettes is to dramatize swiftly and picturesquely Laura's initiation as the mistress of this man; she is at last getting the glamour and the finery her nature has instinctively craved. The automobile show and Reveillon-Freres [the furriers] should be staged with particular regard for showmanship. Possibly we will use a sextette of fur models at Reveillon-Freres. They could pass in revue before Laura and Brockton, with Laura trying on one of the exquisite sables as the climax of the scene.[42]

Although they did not speak directly about decor and costume, the censors were clearly not happy about these scenes. After previewing a rough cut of the film, Joy made an allusion to the problem of luxury, writing to Thalberg that the film does not "bring out contrasting moral values to balance the evident attractions and benefits of the life of a kept woman."[43] "Evident attractions and benefits" would seem to refer to the visual display of cars, furs, and apartments described in the script which must have struck Joy with force upon viewing a print. After the New York censor board reviewed the film, James Wingate made a complaint similar to Joy's. He noted that the heroine is "maintained in wealth and affluence," and that "much of the length of the film is devoted to building up such attractive surroundings."[44] Thus, the problem posed by the liaison between Laura and Brockton was twofold: not only was the sexual relation made too explicit, but also, through the visuals, the terms of exchange.

The negotiations concerning the ending take on significance in this context, for it was by manipulating the ending, and more generally making a point about the film's ultimate "moral effect," that the Studio Relations Committee sought to defend the inclusion of material relating to the sexual liaison. The Code was instrumental throughout this phase of the negotiations. In dealing with the studio, Joy discussed the plot of *The Easiest Way* in terms of the Code directive that "the sympathy of the audience shall never be thrown to the side of crime, wrong-doing, evil or sin." He objects that the (first complete) script brings the audience into sympathy with the heroine's conduct and, for this reason, would "make a motion picture which will not only be a violation of the major tenets of the Code, but will be strongly criticized by that section of the public with which we have to contend as a justification of immorality."[45] He therefore requests that the studio revise the script so as to pass moral judgments on Laura's actions. The revisions suggested are a perfect example of the Studio Relations Committee's routine. He recommends a denunciation scene in which the heroine herself would "make it plain that the life she had been leading had been hideous, destructive, shameful and unhappy."[46] And he requests an ending in which the heroine is punished for her transgressions. In the course of the negotiations, Joy sanctions two endings which adhere to this logic. In the first, Laura is to be alone in the nightclub, as in one of the endings in the original screenplay. This is to be followed by a series of lap dissolves which show her "on her way to the gutter." A second ending had Laura in the shadows, peering in the window at her married sister, Peg. Joy recommended that the studio:

> show the married sister Peg in the happy surroundings of her home and the companionship of her husband and child. Laura, the social outcast, comes to the window and regretfully looks in on the scene of a life that might have been hers. She wants to go in but is afraid to and finally slinks off and is swallowed in the darkness. This scene would set up for the audience a comparison between the happy results of a natural life lived by Peg and the unhappy results of the unconventional life chosen by Laura.[47]

As his language makes clear, Joy looks to the contrast between Peg and Laura to illustrate a moral precept for the spectator.

Without being able to see a print, it is not easy to determine how many of Joy's proposals were actually adopted by the studio. Apparently MGM did not opt to include the denunciation scene (at least, it does not appear in the cutting continuity script). Further, the studio did not immediately conform to either of his suggestions for the ending. A number of other endings were written in late November and early December, which try out various ways of reconciling the couple. These all work by means of a sudden reformation of the heroine. In one, for example, Laura is working in a department store (following a time lapse).[48] In conversation, she warns the other girls against the evils of the "easy" life and affirms the importance of being financially independent. Upon leaving the store, she meets Madison by chance and they are reconciled. The ending adopted in the cutting continuity script is somewhat closer to Joy's preference, although it clearly has been altered through compromise with the studio. As in Joy's ending, Laura peers in the window at her sister Peg, but her brother-in-law discovers her and invites her in. It is Christmas and the family is decorating the tree. It is suggested that when Madison "cools down" he will want to marry her. Thus the studio retains the idea of the formation of the couple as a possibility for the future and, to a degree, softens the irreparable difference between Peg and Laura which Joy sought to emphasize.

While the studio did not conform to the Studio Relations Committee's preference for didactic scenes, there were considerable grounds for agreement between them, and much of what the industry censors wanted to make explicit is given implicitly in the development of the narrative. Consider the denunciation scene which Joy had requested be inserted in the sequence in which Laura falls in love with Madison. The declaration he formulated that life with Brockton had been "hideous, destructive, shameful and unhappy" can be seen as a strategic move to negate or deny the initial attraction to Brockton, or rather the more general appeal of luxury. The final script does not employ this kind of speech, but in establishing the possibility of a legitimate couple (Laura and Madison) it mitigates the terms of Laura's initial rise. The romance is the vehicle of a double moral regeneration: Madison renounces drink and makes plans to resume his career, while Laura plans to support herself while awaiting his return from South America. This arrangement promises the restoration of the moral order—chastity, sobriety, hard work, self-reliance—in and through their union. Thus, the progressive unfolding of the action, the choice of Madison over Brockton, already begins to undo or negate the initial liaison.

Laura's return to Brockton undercuts expectations which are set up by the earlier sequence; it deflects the narrative from the path which seemed to lead toward the coupling of Laura and Madison and the (moral) terms of resolution this implied. Significantly, Laura's return to Brockton was considered much "worse" than the original seduction in the eyes of censors. Joy complained about this sequence that Laura returned "entirely too easily" and asked that the heroine show more resistance.[49] Further, according to MGM's Canadian distributor, the Canadian boards would not permit Laura to return to Brockton at all and it was necessary to delete entire sequences dealing with her return and their living together in his apartment.[50]

The objection to this sequence seems to derive from its narrative placement. Laura's engagement with Madison holds open the promise of an ideal union which is then betrayed by her decision to return to Brockton. The Studio Relations Committee's ending, too, is in part an attempt to compensate for this turn in the plot. Peering in the window at her sister's, Laura enacts a yearning for the domestic paradise which has been lost. Censorship blocks the formation of the couple only to insist the more strongly upon all that it had come to symbolize in the course of the narrative. Of course, the ending in the cutting continuity script attenuates this effect somewhat, since Laura is invited inside, is thus no longer an outcast. But we should not overemphasize the difference between the studio's preferred ending and the censor's. While there is disagreement concerning the fate of the individual character (more or less punishment), there is agreement concerning the general contours of the scene. After experimenting with several possibilities—the speakeasy, the street, the department store—the studio opts for the ending in what the script calls Peg and Nick's "cottage." The final choice of this location is significant since it provides a final tableau of middle-class domesticity, heightened by a religious reference, the image of the family with child on Christmas. This image stands in opposition to Laura's contract with Brockton, in both sexual and economic terms. Quite apart from the question of Laura's punishment, then, the scene serves as a means of negating what has gone before.

I have argued that the ending serves as a means of compensating for Laura's rise in the elaboration of the narrative. In order to delineate the strategic use of endings within the period, however, we must consider the film's reception by the New York state censor board. *The Easiest Way* was apparently one of the first instances in which the MPPDA acted on behalf of the studio in negotiations with the boards.[51] Jason Joy exchanged unusually long and detailed letters with Wingate of the New York board concerning what was acceptable under the Code. Joy writes in defense of two fallen woman films, *The Easiest Way* (MGM) and *Inspiration* (MGM), and two gangster films, *Little Caesar* (Warners) and *See America Thirst* (Universal):

> Always drama has been permitted to paint the unconventional, the
> unlawful, the immoral side of life in order to bring out in immediate
> contrast the happiness and benefits derived from wholesome clean and
> law abiding conduct and thus without actually preaching a sermon

giving the audiences the opportunity of inevitably forming the conclusion that the breaking of human or divine laws brings punishment of some kind. . . . We are sure that it was never intended that censorship should be destructive, picking at details, ignoring the effect of the whole but rather that its duty should be a constructive one of influencing the quality of the final impression left on the minds of the audiences by the whole, irrespective of details possibly objectionable in themselves, sincerely used by the producer as a means of making necessary contrasts. . . . The mere statement or even description of an evil, lawless or immoral act is not in itself immoral and the question of whether it would "tend to corrupt morals" or incite to crime would depend always upon the impression left as to whether the act stated is profitable or unprofitable.[52]

Joy makes a comparison between two possible representations of a murder—one in which the murderer is punished, and the other in which the murderer is acclaimed and congratulated for committing a crime. Only the latter, he argues, tends to corrupt morals. Joy seems to follow the logic of the "Reasons" section of the Code here: film produces moral effects, and censorship must consider and seek to direct such effects. Clearly, however, he raises this argument in order to expand the definition of what is acceptable under the Code. He goes on to defend scenes and lines of dialogue presented in *Little Caesar* and *The Easiest Way* with reference to the "moral" he attributes to the resolution of the stories; to the gangster's death at the end of *Little Caeser* and Laura's final separation from Madison in *The Easiest Way*. His strategy is to reduce consideration of the effect of a film "as a whole" to a consideration of its ending. The representation of any number of elements can be justified if, in the end, crime does not pay.

Wingate's response to Joy's argument is instructive, first, because he discusses the general policy of the New York state board in terms of *The Easiest Way*, and second, because Wingate eventually assumes a position working with Joy on behalf of the industry.[53] He articulates what will become the core of the Studio Relations Committee's regulatory policy regarding the fallen woman and gangster cycles. Wingate agrees with Joy that films can portray "evils" as long as moral judgments are rendered; that is, he agrees with the logic of the "Reasons" section of the Code. In his view, however, this cannot be the board's sole criterion for judgment. "There is of course always the question of whether the alluring evils of life are not overemphasized." *The Easiest Way* is an example of a film in which the moral proposed by the ending is insufficient to counteract the evil portrayed. He proposes to handle the problem of this, and similar, films by "leaving more to influence and imagination, taking out such parts of the dialogue which when eliminated will make the description more delicate." Clearly, then, Joy was not entirely successful in his bid to protect such films from cuts. In his interchange with Wingate, however, the two stake out the areas to be negotiated between them. The fallen woman and gangster cycles were permissible, provided there was some general form of moral commentary, preferably an unhappy ending, and provided some cuts were made that the board would require according to the exigencies of the specific case.

The concerns and policies stated explicitly by Joy and Wingate in this case come to be assumed, or are mentioned only in passing, in later cases. But they constitute the general outlines for negotiations between both the Studio Relations Committee and producers and the Studio Relations Committee and the state boards in this period.

The case of *The Easiest Way* is indicative of the relatively restricted range of narrative options articulated during the process of self-regulation. Many of the revisions suggested by the Studio Relations Committee followed directly from the nineteenth-century traditions of the genre. For example, Joy's recommendation that the film end with a series of short scenes which showed the heroine "on the way to the gutter" is simply a truncated version of the fall. And the scene in which Laura peers in the window at her sister's happy family evokes the same sense of nostalgia and remorse as Rossetti's painting *The Gate of Memory,* or the denouement of *East Lynne,* in which the fallen woman sneaks back into her former household, to peer at her sleeping child.

Not only did censorship rely on genre conventions, but also it is clear that censorship built upon narrative tendencies apparent in "uncensored" scripts. For example, even in the original draft of *The Easiest Way,* the heroine's rise is softened and more or less normalized when she falls in love and tries to reform for Madison. The Studio Relations Committee simply wanted to cast this emphasis on the couple in a more punitive tone, with the heroine finally definitively excluded from all possibility of redemption, defined as heterosexual romance. Thus, the strategies of censorship relied upon a configuration of the couple which was already conventionalized within the Hollywood cinema, and given, to a degree, in the scripts it took under consideration.

A question which remains, then, is why censorship in this period was relatively unsuccessful in its own terms, that is, unable to prevent the release of films which proved unacceptable to the boards and offensive in the public sphere. The case of *The Easiest Way* suggests that in practice the Production Code provided great leeway for negotiations between both the Studio Relations Committee and producers and the Studio Relations Committee and the state boards. These negotiations allowed for, and perhaps even encouraged, the development of rhetorical techniques for slipping material which had been defined as potentially offensive past the censor. Self-regulation was relatively unsystematic, confined to details or privileged but isolated moments such as a film's ending. The next two chapters demonstrate some of the ways in which it was possible to bypass these constraints; to utilize indirect modes of representation to suggest what could not be directly said or shown, and to develop the narrative as a whole in ways which violated the sense of the ending.

3

Glamour and Gold Diggers

JAMES WINGATE ALLUDES to the problem of Laura's "attractive surroundings" in *The Easiest Way*, but he does not explain what he objects
to in terms of specific images. Reformers complain about the "glamour"
associated with the fallen woman, but they use the term as if its meaning
were self-evident, without reference to concrete examples. An investigation of the concept of glamour is thus crucial if we are to pinpoint what
aspects of the films offended viewers and why industry censors often
found themselves unable to modulate representations of female sexuality
sufficiently to protect the industry.

Nineteenth-century versions of the fallen woman story traditionally
characterized the courtesan by her excessive levels of expenditure and
rich, quasi-aristocratic life-style. For example, Zola describes Nana's
bedchamber after she has become the mistress of the wealthy Count
Muffat as follows:

On the elaborately upholstered bed, which was as low as a sofa, there
were twenty thousand francs'-worth of *point de Venise* lace. The
furniture was lacquered blue and white under designs in silver filigree;
and everywhere lay such numbers of white bearskins that they hid the
carpet. This was a luxurious caprice on Nana's part, she having never
been able to break herself of the habit of sitting on the floor to take
her stockings off. Next door to the bedroom the little saloon was full of
an amusing medley of exquisitely artistic objects. Against the hangings
of pale rose-coloured silk—a faded Turkish rose-colour, embroidered
with gold thread—a whole world of them stood sharply outlined. They
were from every land and in every possible style. There were Italian
cabinets, Spanish and Portuguese coffers, models of Chinese pagodas,
a Japanese screen of precious workmanship, besides china, bronzes,
embroidered silks, hangings of the finest needlework. Armchairs wide
as beds, and sofas deep as alcoves, suggested voluptuous idleness and
the somnolent life of the seraglio. The prevailing tone of the room was
old gold, blended with green and red, and nothing it contained too

forcibly indicated the presence of the courtesan save the luxuriousness of the seats.[1]

But while the fallen woman has often been represented as living in luxury, "glamour" in the films cannot be explained simply as an elaboration of prior genre conventions. In order to appreciate the force of Hollywood's treatment of the luxury motif we need to consider a host of representational practices specific to the film industry: uses of mise-en-scène which called attention to the fallen woman's wealth and style, forms of publicity which helped to reinforce an interest in fashion and set design.

During the teens, the studio system had developed in ways which permitted the creation of complex and costly sets. Budgets for settings gradually increased in this period, positions such as that of the art director were created, and the use of back lots and standing sets became commonplace.[2] This system allowed for the construction of settings typical of the fallen woman film, such as elegant hotel suites, bathrooms and dressing rooms, and penthouse apartments. These settings were frequently rendered in the manner of Cedric Gibbons' art department at MGM: "mercilessly white, every bedroom a ballroom and every ballroom a palace."[3] Such settings were also often aggressively "modern." In the twenties, stories about flappers and fallen women provided a showcase for experimentation in set design. After attending the influential 1925 Paris Exposition des Arts Décoratifs, Cedric Gibbons decided to exploit the new design trends in a trilogy of films which concerned the sexual mores of the young generation: *Our Dancing Daughters, Our Modern Maidens,* and *Our Blushing Brides*[4] (see Figures 3.1 and 3.2). Richard Dey, who actually planned the sets for these films, went on to design *The Kiss,* also in the deco style, about a married woman who has a love affair, and eventually kills her husband. Like Gibbons and Dey, Van Nest Polglase, who became supervising art director at RKO, made his reputation on ultramodern sets for two films, *Untamed* and *The Magnificent Flirt,* which dealt with sexually emancipated women.[5]

In the twenties, the kinds of design typical of the genre were noted by reviewers and even censors; perhaps because the settings looked unusual, they were hard to ignore. A *New York Times* reviewer commented that *The Magnificent Flirt* subscribed to "modernistic conceptions of furnishings."[6] The secretary who reported on *Our Modern Maidens* for the National Board of Review complained that the film, "a

3.1 *Our Dancing Daughters*. The living room set.

3.2 *Our Dancing Daughters*. The bedroom set.

portrayal of excessively modern maidens," also had "extremely modern" settings.[7] By the early thirties, the association between the fallen woman and art moderne was so well established that it was exploited as a part of a film's advertising campaign. The press kit for *The Greeks Had a Word for Them* advised exhibitors to decorate their lobbies in a "modernistic" black and silver color scheme: "Since most of the scenes photographed in the picture show modernistic furnishings in the apartment of the gold diggers, it is therefore in keeping with the general theme of the picture."[8]

While the tendency to associate the fallen woman and architectural modernism continued in the thirties, the sets of this period are sparer and more streamlined, in keeping with the design trends of the decade.[9] For example, consider the penthouse from *Susan Lenox: Her Fall and Rise*, which is discussed at length in Donald Albrecht's study of modern architecture and the movies[10] (see Figure 3.3). The apartment is characterized by the open, easy flow of spaces adopted from the international style of architecture. Antechamber, living room, and terrace form a

3.3 *Susan Lenox*. The penthouse set.

continuum, with distinct areas marked off by a system of raised platforms
and dropped beams. Large glass windows reveal a view of Manhattan
outside and contribute to the sense of openness. The white fireplace
block is ornamented with simple parallel lines, a common deco motif.
Furnishings include streamlined chairs with semicircular sides, and
glass topped tables.

Albrecht argues that the design of the fallen woman film had a
specific narrative function. As a metaphor for modernity, architectural
modernism was associated with the "new" woman, with independence,
sexual promiscuity, and feminine self-indulgence. He notes:

> Modern design came to be associated with forces that were threatening
> domestic security: The technologically advanced kitchen which might
> free women to pursue activities outside the home was lampooned,
> while the bedroom and the bathroom became natural backdrops
> for loose-living women who had turned their backs on homemaking
> and indulged themselves in a life of pleasure.[11]

Similarly, in a book on art deco and cinema, Howard Mandelbaum and
Eric Myers point out that the fallen woman's penthouse was often con-
trasted with the more traditional decor associated with the "good" woman,
that is, the ideal of domesticity.[12] A somewhat different opposition seems
to have structured the use of the moderne style in *The Easiest Way,* however. The heroine acquires a moderne penthouse, complete with tubular
furniture, and a glass-walled nook in which she eats breakfast overlooking
the city. The script and the extant production stills suggest a contrast
between this set and that of the opening of the film, in which the heroine
and her impoverished family eat breakfast in cramped and dreary surroundings (see Figures 3.4 and 3.5). In this opposition, modernism functions to signal the fashionable nature of the fallen woman's new surroundings. Industry censors and reformers were in part reacting to this
usage of architectural modernism in their complaints about glamour. Although the terms in which Jason Joy and James Wingate speak about the
attractiveness of the fallen woman's life-style are vague, one of the things
they must have found overly attractive, and hence objectionable, was the
style in which Laura's apartment was portrayed.

Alongside architectural design, clothes played an important role in
designating the fallen woman's status. A number of historians have
pointed to the confluences between the film, fashion, and advertising

3.4 *The Easiest Way.* The tenement set.

industries which first emerged in the twenties. For example, Lary May has noted that much of the publicity about stars in the teens was concerned with their apparel and cosmetics.[13] Writing about the thirties, Charles Eckert has demonstrated how the display of fashions became institutionalized in the form of advertising tie-ins and promotions which showcased costumes for particular features.[14] In this context, the display of clothes became highly conventionalized within the fallen woman film, and was accorded a prominent narrative function.

The films define class through fashion, rather than through work or the evocation of a shared cultural milieu. A relatively restricted set of items—furs, jewels, orchids, sequined gowns—serve as signs of wealth and power within the genre. In *Easy Living* (1937), for example, a wealthy industrialist throws his wife's fur coat out of the window of their penthouse apartment. It falls on the head of a working girl on the street below. Her possession of the coat is interpreted by the manager of a luxury hotel as a sign that she is the industrialist's mistress. The man-

3.5 *The Easiest Way.* The penthouse set.

ager provides her with a suite of rooms and other favors, assuming he will be amply repayed. This representation of class rise borders on the fantastic. An extraordinary, almost magical power is attached to the fur, insofar as it has the power instantly to redefine the heroine's class identity and moral standing within the world of the story.

Easy Living is one of a very large number of Cinderella stories which deal with the motif of mistaken class identity, that is, in which lower-class characters pass themselves off as rich (alternatively, upper-class characters are mistaken for lower-class ones in the course of the narrative). Class identity is thus subject to swift and far-reaching transformations, accomplished almost at will. Disguise, the calculated display of clothes and jewels, is the medium of these alterations in status. In *Footloose Widows* (1926), for example, two models steal wardrobes from the agency at which they work. They travel to Florida, where they pose as wealthy widows in the hopes of catching rich husbands. They seek to entrap an elegantly attired gentleman, who turns out to be in disguise too, only a poor newspaperman on the make. Through the plot device of disguise, then, class becomes a labile and manipulable category. A shimmering gown or a top hat enables characters to move at will into and out of upper-class settings. The boundaries of class difference, often quite marked at the beginning of these stories, are crossed repeatedly and ultimately transcended without any hint of work, struggle, or resentment between classes.

Like the motif of disguise, what I call transformation scenes served to dramatize social mobility. In its simplest form, the transformation consists in two or more consecutive scenes in which the heroine acquires new clothes. Sometimes she also receives an automobile, the modern-day equivalent of the carriage that the fairy godmother bestowed on Cinderella. As we have seen, the first completed draft of the script of *The Easiest Way* calls for a series of short scenes intended to "dramatize swiftly and picturesquely Laura's initiation as the mistress of this man; [that] she is at last getting the glamour and the finery her nature has instinctively craved."[15] These scenes are emphasized in the production stills which MGM prepared for the film (see Figures 3.6 and 3.7). The

3.6 *The Easiest Way.* Publicity still.

3.7 *The Easiest Way*. Publicity still.

heroine's transformation can also occur in scenes which are spaced out
across the course of the film. In this case, composition, framing, and
lighting call attention to the changes in her mode of dress and living. *Baby
Face*, to be discussed in detail below, clearly fits within this tradition,
tracing Lily's transformation from her slovenly appearance in the speakeasy, through her fashionable secretarial attire, to the jewels and gown
which she acquires as a wealthy, married woman (see Figures 3.8–3.10).

Transformation scenes posed real problems for the Studio Relations
Committee in that the heroine's glamorous look resulted unmistakably
from an exchange of sex for money. While industry censors repeatedly
sought to delete or attenuate moments in which women bargained with
men or money changed hands, they were unable to affect the kinds of
visual display which, in their view, rendered such exchanges admirable
and attractive to audiences. Thus, in *The Easiest Way*, censors delete the
dialogue in which Brockton promises Laura a life of luxury, but they do
not even contemplate changing the penthouse set or the shopping scenes
in which this luxury is manifested.

3.8 *Baby Face*. Lily at her father's speakeasy.

3.9 *Baby Face*. Lily as a bank secretary.

3.10 *Baby Face*. Lily as the wife of the bank president.

Like transformation scenes, what might loosely be called the tradition of glamour photography helped to propagate an awareness of style,
and provided a catalogue of particular images which could be mobilized
within given narrative contexts to adorn, motivate, even justify illicit
sexuality. Charles Eckert notes that it became routine for the studios to
publicize features through posters, lobby displays, and photographs distributed in fan magazines, women's magazines, and department stores.
While many of these photographs emphasized the face of the star in
close-up, others were designed to show off the costumes and settings
depicted in the films.[16]

The campaign proposed in the press book for *The Greeks Had a Word
for Them* (1932) is a good example of how glamour photographs could
work against the impetus of censorship. Adapted from a play by Zoe
Atkins, the script, in the judgment of Lamar Trotti, was not acceptable
film material.[17] Hays himself attempted to dissuade Samuel Goldwyn
from producing it and was involved in negotiations on retakes and re-
editing of the rough cut.[18] Certainly, part of the problem with the script
was the storyline. Because it was a farce, *The Greeks Had a Word for
Them* did not allow for the tragic endings or moral didacticism which

censors preferred. Alongside these difficulties of plot, however, censors were concerned about the visual portrayal of luxury. For example, Trotti complained to Goldwyn that "with them [the gold diggers] prostitution has become a fine art, with beautiful jewels, and all the comforts of life as the rewards of their activities. . . . In other words, these three young women make immorality pay handsomely."[19] The publicity campaign proposed for the film served to underscore the luxury associated with the three protagonists.[20] "All gowns designed by Chanel of Paris, the greatest fashion show on earth," read one advertising slogan. Exhibitors were offered a set of eight-by-ten "fashion photographs" for display in their lobbies. They were further advised to plant the stills in shop windows and the fashion columns of local newspapers. Included with each package of stills was a detailed description of the garments shown in the photographs, as an aid for fashion editors and newspaper columnists. Exhibitors could also make arrangements with the studio-sponsored Modern Merchandising Bureau to have samples of merchandise and appropriate window display material, including photographs of the stars in costume, sent directly to stores in their neighborhoods.

While censors had asked the screenwriters to play up the character of Polaire, on the grounds that she was the most redeemable of the threesome,[21] the preponderance of publicity photographs are of Ina Claire, who played the rapacious Jean. Some of the publicity stills of Claire go so far as to hint at some sort of sexual impropriety. In the photographs which showcase her ring and fur coat, for example, she assumes a wry and knowing look, as if to emphasize the ring's illicit origins (see Figure 3.11). Even if one hasn't seen the film, such an image evokes a whole narrative of promise and exchange. Most of the stills do not suggest a narrative, however. She is photographed against abstract backdrops, posing to show off her clothes and jewelry (see Figures 3.12 and 3.13). While not as narratively loaded as the photograph of Claire in the fur, these relatively "straight" publicity photographs also worked against the interests of censorship; they reinforced the allure of the heroine's status simply by accenting and reinforcing subtle nuances of design.

Censorship thus confronted powerful countervailing forces. The morally didactic tone approved by industry censors, and more generally, the overall tenor of nineteenth-century genre conventions, were consistently at odds with what I have described as a preoccupation with class rise, defined in terms of opportunities for consumption and celebrated through

3.11 *The Greeks Had a Word for Them.* Publicity still.

display. Such display consisted in part of specific props: the furs, automobiles, and jewels which served as signs of upper-class status. It also
comprised the design of particular spaces: modernist penthouses, night-
clubs, or luxury hotels in which the harmonies of color, shape, and form
often set off the heroine's clothes and helped to foreground the very idea
of fashion. Moreover, the advertising network of the studio system,
which promoted female stars on the basis of their clothes, cosmetics, and
jewels, gave institutional support to the aura of glamour which surrounded the fallen women.

Baby Face

The Studio Relations Committee did not affect these elements of glamour. Censors did not routinely review set or costume design. While film
posters were subject to self-regulation under the terms of the industry's
Advertising Code, glamour photographs of the stars were not censored as
such.[22] The representation of class rise became a target for regulation,

3.12 *The Greeks Had a Word for Them.* Publicity still.

3.13 *The Greeks Had a Word for Them.* Publicity still.

then, only in those cases in which a woman actively sought to acquire finery by illicit means. This was most often the case in gold-digger films. Gold diggers are active, controlling characters; they explicitly propose to exploit their sexuality for jewels and real estate. Not only did this characterization foreground a more general tendency to glamorize the heroine, but also, it associated the scenario of class rise with a representation of female sexuality which the industry's critics found especially repugnant.

Many gold-digger films, including *Bed of Roses, Red Headed Woman, Baby Face, The Greeks Had a Word for Them, She Done Him Wrong,* and *I'm No Angel,* would probably be classified as comedies by most film critics, and hence at the perimeters of the fallen woman genre, properly conceived as a subset of melodrama. Industry censors, however, classified comedies like *The Greeks Had a Word for Them* as "sex pictures," in tandem with films like *Madame X* which we would consider pure melodrama. Indeed, they gave much attention to the ways in which comedy could be used for strategic purposes, as a means of justifying otherwise unacceptable material. These films are thus interesting precisely because they crossed the boundary between comedy and melodrama. Their comedy frequently derives from a parodic inversion of genre conventions. They played havoc with the traditional characterization of the fallen woman, and the corresponding notions of innate feminine passivity and innocence.

The opening of *Possessed* is a good example of a comic permutation of the fall. The heroine works in a paper box factory in a small town. She is reluctant to accept the marriage proposed by a local construction worker and dreams of bettering herself. Standing by the railroad tracks at night, she looks in the windows of a passing train and sees a series of tableaux which represent the allure of the city: in one window, a couple kiss; in another, a man in a tux shakes a pitcher of cocktails; in a third, servants press evening clothes. On the last boxcar on the train she encounters an elegantly dressed man, slightly drunk on champagne. He begins to flirt with her, the dialogue self-consciously referring to the convention of the country girl seduced by the enticements of the city: "Could city slicker tempt country girl with liquor?" He advises her to go off to the city, "to be done wrong by." The comedy of the scene results from the fact that, to his dismay, she is not unwilling. He complains: "Don't tell me you are not a country maiden with a heart of gold beating beneath your flannel nightie. I can't bear it. . . . This is not working out right. You should be blushing like blazes and I should be leering." She eventually takes his advice, arriving on his doorstep in New York, ready, in his words, "to meet a rich man and let nature take its course." Thus, the fall is no longer a question of the corruption or debasement of innocence but rather a stroke of good fortune for a poor girl on the make.

There are many other comic versions of the fall, in which the power relations between the sexes are reversed, and women entrap or trick their supposed seducers. The heroine of *Bed of Roses,* a hard-boiled ex-con, pretends to be a well-bred socialite in order to establish a liaison with a wealthy publisher. She gets him hopelessly drunk and, the next morning, leads him to believe she was seduced, pretending to be a shy and aggrieved innocent. In a mockery of the melodramatic conventions of the cycle, she even threatens suicide. He is thus forced to do the honorable thing, taking her as his mistress and setting her up in a penthouse.

Mae West's *She Done Him Wrong* explicitly signals the way in which it inverts the terms of the fallen woman story. The film introduces a figure who is immediately recognizable as a fallen woman: Sally, exceedingly frail and dressed in poor, ripped clothes, attempts suicide in a saloon. She is carried upstairs into the luxurious boudoir of Diamond Lil (Mae West), where she intimates she is carrying an illegitimate child. Lil sums up the situation as a reprise of a traditional plot: "Some guy done her wrong. The story's so old it should've been set to music long ago." The incident serves to underscore the film's reversal of this sexual dynamic. Lil explains that she has learned to make it in a man's world, a strategy which consists of cheerfully abandoning old lovers when it becomes convenient to do so and making the acquisition of diamonds her career.

Not only is the gold digger calculating and exploitative in her relations with men, she is also sexually knowing, aggressive, and unashamed. In *Red Headed Woman,* the heroine forces her way into her boss's home when his wife is away and seduces him. When he tries to return to his wife, she pursues him avidly, closing him up in a phone booth with her on one occasion and eventually locking him in her bedroom and refusing to relinquish the key. In *The Greeks Had a Word for Them*, the gold digger Jean strips off her dress when she finds herself in the presence of a suitably endowed male prospect. Some of Mae West's most famous lines, which caused the MPPDA no end of grief, rely on the comedienne's unabashedly assuming a sexual posture, as in Diamond Lil's claim to be "one of the finest women who ever walked the streets."[23]

The letters of protest addressed to the MPPDA are extremely vehement on the topic of the aggressive, gold-digging woman. As already noted, Alice Ames Winter, who did public relations work for the MPPDA, writes to Hays of being nauseated by *Bed of Roses*.[24] There are letters from members of various Better Film Societies on the topic of *Red Headed Woman*. One complains: "Sex, sex, sex, the picture just reeks of it. . . . If the Hays Office does not call a halt to pictures such as this, it's going to crystallize such a revulsion of feeling that the industry is going to feel it in no uncertain way."[25] Public reaction to the Mae West films seems to have been divided. An MPPDA publicity report summarizing public opinion on "the Mae West Menace" quotes from several positive reviews. One letter, to a paper in Muncie, Indiana, states: "I was beginning to doubt my sanity as everyone I came in contact with told me how they enjoyed Mae West in *I'm No Angel*."[26] While Mae West was undoubtedly popular, her films were also quite controversial among reform groups. In a personal note to Will Hays, Sidney Kent complained that *She Done Him Wrong* was worse than *Red Headed Woman* and would be detrimental to the industry.[27] Writing to Hays in October of 1935, Breen recommended against Paramount's proposed rerelease of *She Done Him Wrong* and *I'm No Angel,* on the grounds that they would greatly exacerbate the protests being directed at the studios.[28]

Aside from the public controversy they elicited, the gold-digger films were also consistently in trouble with domestic and foreign censor boards. A distribution agent for MGM notes that *Red Headed Woman* was more difficult to get past the Canadian censor boards than a gangster film.[29] RKO was almost unable to distribute *Bed of Roses* in Great Britain and had to prepare a specially amended print for release there.[30] Paramount experienced similar difficulties with *She Done Him Wrong* in Australia and Great Britain. Moreover, all of these films were cut by the state boards within the domestic market; the cuts seem to have been especially severe in Pennsylvania, Ohio, and New York.[31]

I propose to consider the process of self-regulation in some detail in the case of *Baby Face.* The film is of interest because it is clearly a limit case, one which provoked a great deal of comment both inside and outside the industry. Made by Warners in 1933, it was banned in Switzerland, Australia, three Canadian provinces, and in the United States in Virginia, Ohio, and initially New York (where it was later released). It was widely criticized in the popular press and was one of the films listed by Martin Quigley as particularly offensive to the Catholic Legion of Decency.[32] The Studio Relations Committee's failure to protect the industry on this score was not the result of a simple oversight. In the first review of the script, James Wingate, who was working for the industry at this time, warned the studio that the story was likely to run into trouble: "it is exceedingly difficult to get by with the type of story which portrays a woman who, by means of her sex, rises to a position of prominence and luxury."[33] He even cautioned that a film with a similar theme (probably MGM's *Red Headed Woman*) had been banned in several Canadian provinces. Thus, the Studio Relations Committee's difficulty with *Baby Face* did not stem from a difficulty in anticipating the responses of external agencies, but rather lay in the *form* of the revisions enacted according to the Studio Relations Committee's standard operating policy and procedure.

All of the action in the film is motivated by the heroine's rise, and this is intimately linked to the exploitation of men by women. In dealing with the motif of the rise, the Studio Relations Committee followed its usual procedure, seeking to eliminate moments in which the exchange of sex for money was made explicit—in which bargains were struck or money was paid out. Despite these revisions, however, the film continues to emphasize the idea of exchange, utilizing indirect means of representation, specifically camera movement, music, and decor, to figure what cannot be literally said or shown. The Studio Relations Committee also negotiated a number of denunciation scenes, referred to here as the "voice of morality," and a major revision of the ending. I will argue that these changes did not substantively transform the logic of the progression of the narrative. The insistence upon exploitation overrides the sense of the ending, in which the heroine is suddenly and rather inexplicably "reformed."

Baby Face, from a story outline by Darryl Zanuck, was developed into a screenplay by Gene Markey and Katherine Scola.[34] It is not easy to place in terms of genre. Like *Red Headed Woman* or the Mae West films, it indulges in a great deal of sexual innuendo, making jokes about the gold digger's ability to manipulate male desire and prosper at men's expense. But the comic treatment of the gold digger's fall and rise alternates rather oddly with a melodramatic treatment of the fate of the men who are her victims. Not only does Baby Face destroy the men who love her, but she also brings on the failure of the bank at which she works. As Richard Maltby points out, the film's heroine echoes the threatening vamp of the teens, updated by reference to the Depression.[35] The film thus mixes comic and melodramatic elements and is probably one of the most somber of the gold-digger films.

The opening, typical of Warner Brothers in this period, provides an extremely condensed and sensational exposition. Lily Powers works in her father's speakeasy in a steel town in Pennsylvania. There is an unusually frank antagonism between Lily and her father, Nick, which takes the form of "hard-boiled" dialogue, taunts, insults. The action is initiated when Sipple, a crooked politician who gives the speakeasy "protection," hands Nick twenty dollars to clear the bar and leave him alone with Lily. Lily resists Sipple's advances, and he angrily departs after she hits him over the head with a beer bottle. The ensuing argument between Lily and her father is interrupted by the report that Nick's still is on fire (an "accident" attributed to the loss of Sipple's protection). Lily watches while Nick is killed in an explosion trying to put out the blaze.

After Nick's death, Lily visits her one friend in town, the cobbler Cragg. He advises her to go to New York and "make something" of herself. In a rather bizarre citation, he reads from Nietzsche's *The Will to Power*, here used as a kind of self-help manual, or at least a statement of the gold-digger's code: "All life, no matter how we idealize it, is nothing more nor less than exploitation." Cragg advises Lily that her beauty gives her power over men and she should exploit them for her own ends.

The cobbler's speech initiates the lengthy and episodic sequence concerning the heroine's rise. Hitching a ride to New York in a boxcar, Lily is discovered by a company official who threatens to throw her off the train. She seduces him in order to continue her journey. In New York she obtains a job in a bank by seducing an office boy. She moves up the ranks by seducing other employees: a junior clerk, a section manager, a young executive, and finally his boss, the vice-president. All of these episodes share the same structure. Lily uses her current lover as a stepping stone to the next (and richer) one. Each new conquest entails the betrayal of a former lover and frequently his ruin. The section manager, for example, loses his job because of his liaison with Lily. Lily's rise is unchecked until she tries to move from Stevens, the young executive, to Carter, the vice-president. Stevens shows up at her penthouse one night with a gun, finds Carter in a back room, shoots the vice-president, and then commits suicide.

Threatening to publish the story of her affair with Carter, Lily attempts to blackmail the bank's board of directors for a large sum. She is thwarted by Trenholm, the new president, who tricks her into taking a job in the bank's Paris branch in lieu of a cash payment. After a time lapse, Trenholm meets Lily in Paris and he, too, is attracted to her. But, in an inversion of the earlier seduction scenes, Lily withholds her sexual favors, and thus leads Trenholm to propose marriage. After the wedding, the couple returns to New York to find there has been a run on Trenholm's bank. He asks his wife for the loan of the jewels and stock options she has received from him. Lily refuses, explaining that she is not "soft" like other women, and makes plans to leave him and return to Europe. Before her ship embarks, however, she has a sudden change of heart and rushes back into the city. The original ending is missing from the first draft of the script, but a letter of James Wingate leads me to believe that she finds Trenholm dead, a suicide. A letter of a later date, however,

complains that the ending has been changed, and that Trenholm sur-
vives.[36] I have not found a written version of this, but believe that
Wingate refers to what becomes the penultimate scene in the final print,
in which we see Trenholm in an ambulance. Lily, neglectful of her box
of jewels, waits anxiously at his side. Still another ending—a "tag"—
was added after the film was rejected by the New York state board.[37]

The process of self-regulation was rather involved in this case. James
Wingate reviewed the final draft of the script, but then seems to have
expended most of his efforts in negotiations on the rough cut. After the
film was rejected by the New York state board on April 1, 1933, Warners
withheld it from general release. Will Hays, who viewed it on his annual
trip to the West Coast, met with Jack Warner and Hal Wallis, who agreed
to make further revisions.[38] A new round of negotiations was initiated,
including not only Wingate but Joseph Breen. Some new scenes were
shot, including a new ending, and the film was reedited. Since so much
of the negotiations concerned the film itself, and not the script, it is
unfortunate that I cannot reconstruct the way it looked in the various
stages of editing. However, it is possible to make some deductions about
the content of these negotiations, based upon the script, the Studio
Relations Committee's correspondence with the studio, and the final
release print.

In almost every letter written to Darryl Zanuck, the producer of *Baby
Face*, James Wingate warns that the film is likely to run into trouble with
the boards. In spite of these forebodings, he approved the December
script, on the basis of the ending in which Lily loses Trenholm, and with
the proviso that Warners was to insure that the "details" of the story were
"handled with care and taste." Prior to the film's rejection by the New
York board, most of the negotiations between the Studio Relations Committee and the studio concerned the treatment of "details" of action and
dialogue. Wingate's aim, in this regard, was to avoid the explicit representation of the episodes which compose the rise. He writes:

> As to the treatment of the relationships existing between Lily and each
> of her different men, we believe that insofar as possible you are to
> avoid making the facts of each relationship too explicit. This can be
> done by never really showing through dialogue or action that the man
> in each case is really paying for her apartment, supplying Lily with
> money and clothes in return for her affection.[39]

The film was to be defended, then, on the grounds that it did not literally show what it repeatedly suggests.

In the correspondence with the studio, I have found references to several cuts which suggest the kinds of revisions Wingate advocated while the film was being edited. For example, he asked the studio to eliminate a shot from the rough cut in which Nick accepts twenty dollars from Sipple, the politician.[40] In Wingate's view, the shot of money changing hands was too direct an indication of the deal between the men. He also encouraged the studio to extend ellipses which had already been indicated in the December script. For example, he complained about the conclusion of the scene in which Lily seduces the office boy; the boy follows her into a vacant office and the door closes (of course, the action inside the room is not shown).[41] This is altered in the final release print. The boy watches Lily walk away but does not leave his desk. In effect, the amount of action which is elided has been increased. While the dialogue (they discuss the fact that the room is empty) and the use of point-of-view shots (there is a shot of him looking at her as she moves toward the empty room) indicate that he may be disposed to follow, we do not see him actually initiate this action.

Another difficulty in the use of ellipsis was the scene in which Lily seduces a train official.[42] As in the scene in the office, the problem was the concluding shot, which called attention to the elided action. The final shot of the scene is a close-up in which the man's gloves fall to the floor of the boxcar and his lantern is extinguished. The close-up limits our vision but at the same time isolates a detail which emphasizes what remains offscreen. Wingate requested the elimination of the final close-up, and, after the film was rejected by the New York state board, the whole episode was deleted from the release print.

Wingate's preoccupation with the scenes in the office and on the train brings up the larger problem of sexual innuendo. When Wingate writes that the episodes of Lily's climb must be treated with "good taste," he is advocating the use of ellipsis and other indirect modes of representation in the seduction scenes. However, this strategy does not necessarily preclude sly, indirect suggestions of sexual activity: jokes which observe, indeed presuppose, the limitations of censorship even as they circumvent these limits. Industry censors frequently seem to have accepted such jokes as a routine part of their operating procedure. Consider the Studio Relations Committee's treatment of Ernst Lubitsch's comedies, renowned for indirect, sexually suggestive shots. In the case of *One Hour with You,* Joy notes that he is willing to permit the production to proceed without objection, despite the unmistakable intimation that the hero commits adultery, "because the director and cast can handle risqué scenes with tact and good taste."[43] Again, in the case of *Trouble in Paradise,* Joy notes that "the light Lubitsch touch is rather the all-governing factor insofar as domestic censorship is concerned."[44] In contrast with their attitude toward the Lubitsch comedies, industry censors seem to be much less willing to allow for sexual innuendo in *Baby Face.* Wingate's unusual caution in this instance may have derived from the fact that he did not trust the director, Al Green, to be as subtle as Lubitsch. Also, clearly, given the film's theme, he foresaw trouble with the state boards. That is, censorship was directed not at the suggestion of sexual activity per se, but rather at the idea of the woman instigating this activity. Innuendo became a topic of much more stringent negotiation and concern in this case because the seduction scenes carried with them the implication of feminine aggressivity.

Once *Baby Face* was rejected by the New York state board, it became apparent to the MPPDA that Wingate's initial strategy of concentrating on the problem of sexual innuendo was not enough to render the figure of the gold digger acceptable to state censors. The New York board argued that the film was unacceptable because the "story as a whole and the philosophy back of it contravened the New York statute."[45] The board's objection to the film's "philosophy" refers to the use of Nietzsche. This point is clarified in a memo written by Hays after concluding negotiations with Warners on the film. He notes that he "explained fully the situation, the necessity of eliminating the declaration of the Nietzsche philosophy and sufficiently eliminating the practice else the picture could not be shown."[46] The problem, then, was not only the references to *The Will to Power,* but also the idea of exploitation as given abstractly by means of the citations of Nietzsche and as it was worked out through the various episodes of Lily's rise.

Although the cobbler's dialogue was easily eliminated, censors ultimately did not succeed in effacing the idea of exploitation as such. This is because the film utilizes indirect means of representation, so that the idea remains implicit much of the time. Specifically, camera movement, decor, and music are integrated within a system of repetition which conveys the circumstances of Lily's rise. When Lily first arrives in New York, she stands on the sidewalk, poor and bedraggled, and looks up at the skyscraper that houses the bank. When Lily gets her first job, and later, each time she accomplishes another seduction, a shot of the skyscraper is repeated. The camera tilts up the building, "climbing" to the next level she has worked up to. After her marriage to Trenholm, the bank president, the camera moves all the way up to the penthouse on top of another skyscraper. Thus, although we do not see Lily actually receive the promotions, clothes, or other favors, the process of exchange is played out through the visual metaphor of the movement up the building.

The use of music elaborates on this metaphor. The camera movement is accompanied by a honkytonk rendition of "St. Louis Woman" or, in one sequence, "Baby Face." This type of music is particularly associated with the idea of prostitution. Honkytonk piano is twice connected with the atmosphere of the speakeasy. First, in the opening sequence, the confrontation with Sipple is accompanied by piano. And again, later in the film, Lily refuses a gift of a piano, saying that she used to hear one all day long. Further, the lyrics of "St. Louis Woman," which are sung twice during the course of the film, are explicitly related to questions of sexuality and exchange:

> St. Louis Woman
> She got a diamond ring
> Leads that man of mine
> By the apron strings.

What I find interesting here is not simply that music or camera movement can allude to Lily's becoming rich, but also that these elements constitute a system of repetition which propels the narrative forward. The music and camera work connect disparate scenes—the prostitution of Lily in the speakeasy, the seductions at the bank, the marriage—and infuse them all with the unmistakable impetus of the rise. The idea of exploitation is relatively impervious to revision, then, because it is not located in any one scene or line of dialogue, but is gradually accrued, as later scenes are referred back to earlier ones across multiple levels of signification.

In correspondence with the studio, James Wingate tacitly admits that the idea of exploitation remains dominant. He refers to "the philosophy now in the picture, even though Nietzsche has been deleted, namely, use your body for material advancement. . . ."[47] Given this difficulty, Wingate has two suggestions for making the film acceptable to the boards.

These follow predictably from Studio Relations Committee policy and procedure. First, he wants the cobbler to function as what he calls a "voice of morality," to scold the heroine and denounce her "philosophy and mode of life." Second, he wants an unhappy ending. Although he is prepared to let Trenholm survive the suicide attempt, he wants Lily "stripped of her wealth and social standing."[48]

One can make sense of the second round of revisions proposed by Wingate in terms of the Code directive that films must safeguard the moral standards of audiences. The revisions are clearly designed to fulfill a didactic function. For example, under the guise of having the cobbler lecture the heroine, the film addresses a warning about her course of action to the spectator. Considered as a statement of principle, however, the amended dialogue is not at all explicit. The cobbler's criticisms of the heroine tend to be vague and open to broad interpretation, e.g., she is warned against taking the "wrong way." Thus I would argue that the strategy of defense employed here does not rely solely on the "moral" supposedly inculcated. In my view, the revisions serve a compensatory function. That is, their strategic value becomes apparent when we consider them in relation to the idea of exploitation, which was the central point of negotiation and difficulty. In this regard, the revisions seem to me to play a part in the elaboration of the film's sexual problematic; they work to disguise or obscure the guiding theme of the exploitation of men by women.

It is instructive to compare the cobbler's original citation of Nietzsche with the speech given in the final release print. In the script he says:

> A woman—young, beautiful—like you—can get anything she wants in the world! Because you have a power over men! But you must use men—not let them use you! You must be a master, not a slave! . . . Nietzsche says "All life, no matter how we idealize it, is nothing more or less than exploitation!" That's what I'm telling you! Exploit yourself! . . . Use men to get the things you want!

The final release print provides a more conventional view of how to succeed:

> A woman, young, beautiful, like you are, could get anything she wants in the world. But there is a right and a wrong way. Remember the

price of the wrong way is too great. Go to the big city. There you will find opportunities. Don't let people mislead you. You must be a master—not a slave. Be clean, be strong, be defiant and you will be a success.

The revised version contains traces of the original, the distinction between master and slave, the Nietzschean category of the "strong." What has been eliminated, however, is the overt connection between power and female sexuality, phrases such as "use men" and "you have power over men." Moreover, the two speeches perform somewhat different roles in the elaboration of the next sequence. The original speech poses a question or enigma—can Lily exert power over men?—which initiates and to an extent motivates her rise at the bank. The revised dialogue poses an enigma of another order. The question is a moral one—will Lily preserve her virtue in the big city or will she succumb to the temptation of the wrong (easiest) way? But this is a false enigma since, at least after her first conquest, Lily's virtue is never in doubt. The point of suspense throughout her career at the bank is not whether or not she will be seduced, but whether or not the men will be seduced and what this will get her. Thus, the revised version of the cobbler's speech cloaks or denies the sexual dynamic in which the woman is the aggressor and the man her dupe or victim.

There is also a marked change in the way the cobbler is used in relation to the scene of the murder and Stevens' suicide. In the screenplay, Lily receives a letter from the cobbler which contains quotations from Nietzsche's *Thoughts Out of Season:* "Face life as you find it, defiantly and unafraid. Don't waste energy yearning for the moon. Crush out all sentiment." In the release print, she receives a "self-help" book and a letter warning that she should reform: "From your letters I can tell that my advice was for nothing. You have chosen the wrong way. You are still a coward. Life will defeat you unless you fight back and regain your self respect." The letter operates as a framing device for the scene of the murder/suicide. And the revised letter disguises precisely those elements of the scene which the original emphasized.

The visuals of the murder scene suggest that Lily is indifferent to the fate of the men. Shots are heard offscreen as Lily is shown in medium close-up (see Figure 3.14). There is no noticeable alteration of her features. As she approaches the bodies to look at them, she turns quite slowly to reveal her face to the camera. It displays no emotion (see

3.14 *Baby Face*

Figure 3.15). The expressionless close-up is repeated, this time in pro-
file, as she calls the police. By a logic of association, the original version
of the cobbler's letter explains the impassivity of the close-ups as a
gesture of willed indifference, the direct embodiment of the aphorism
"Crush out all sentiment." In contrast, the revised version of the letter
initiates a disjuncture between the writing and visuals of the murder
scene. The letter stresses the heroine's ultimate moral weakness ("Life
will defeat you unless you fight back and regain your self respect"). In
effect, it foretells the end of the story, in which Lily is "defeated," and
must give up her entire fortune. Thus it softens or offsets the effect of the
visuals by anticipating the moment in which she loses control, as if
punishing her, in advance, for her indifference.

The ending is crucial to censorship, not only because it inverts the
trajectory of class rise, but also because the heroine's sudden reformation allows the inversion of the power relations that have been played out
along the lines of sexual difference. Even in the studio's original version
of the ending, a reversal of Lily's coldness and cynicism was necessary
to permit the reconciliation of the couple. Lily rushes back into the city
and, hysterical, declares she is ready to "sacrifice everything" for Tren-

3.15 *Baby Face*

holm. The amended ending heightens this emphasis upon sacrifice and with it, the couple. The final scene is a meeting of the board of directors of the bank. One of the directors announces that Trenholm is alive and that he and his wife have "sacrificed everything they had for the bank." The point is made, at length, that they have no money and that Trenholm is working as a laborer in a steel mill. The dialogue stresses not only Lily's impoverishment, but also her domestication. She is consistently referred to as Mrs. Trenholm (quite a change from Lily Powers), and her class status is aligned with her husband's: "They haven't a cent. He's working as a laborer in the steel mill. They are working out their happiness together." Although Wingate initially objected to the ending in which Trenholm survived, one can see how the formation of the couple works here, along with the heroine's punishment, as part of a general movement which negates and undoes the image of the gold digger as exploitative, indifferent to men.

Thus, the kind of ending preferred by the studio, and typical of the classical cinema, functions as part of a strategy of censorship. But in spite of this rapprochement between the studio and the Studio Relations Committee, we have ample testimony to the inadequacies of censorship in this case—the complaints of the Catholic Legion of Decency for example, and the actions of the other state censor boards, many of which required cuts above and beyond the changes made for New York. The weakness of censorship lies in the fact that, aside from the ending, it is not very well integrated into the narrative sequence. Everything points to the inevitability of Lily's rise. Even the turn in the plot which puts Lily's success in question—the murder/suicide—is resolved in her favor: she is sent to Paris where Trenholm falls in love with her. This emphasis is pushed to the point where the couple itself, the heroine's stereotypical reformation in the name of "true love," is put in question. This is most evident in the sequence in Paris, in which Trenholm is led to propose.

This scene is certainly more romantic in tone than the earlier seductions at the bank. It is set on Trenholm's yacht, with lights reflecting off the water, and instead of the usual jazz accompaniment, a waltz is played by strings. Trenholm complains that Lily leaves him every night "outside the door of the stateroom." As proof of his affection, he offers her diamonds, cars, houses in Paris and New York. Lily rejects this offer on the grounds that it is "not love," and she brings up the idea of marriage, saying, "I want a 'Mrs.' on my tombstone." There are certainly sentimental aspects to Lily's posture: the refusal to barter sex for goods, the reference to death. But her motives remain ambiguous throughout the scene, and it is possible to read them in terms of exploitation. This interpretation remains open, in part, because of the use of close-ups. The actress does not appear at all moved. She looks offscreen, away from the man, and her face is blank. Such an interpretation also rests upon the structural parallel between this scene and the earlier flirtations at the bank: in spite of the differences of setting, this is yet another instance in which Lily trades on male desires, bringing her rise to its culmination. This reading of Lily's motives is capped by the camera movement up the skyscraper, appearing after the couple returns to New York, which underscores the parallel between the marriage and the affairs at the bank.

We are given a system of repetition, then, in which the relations between the sexes are constructed as exploitative, and in which the sentimental posture, "true love," becomes exceedingly ambiguous. To be sure the revisions negotiated by the Studio Relations Committee functioned to attenuate this representation of the cold, calculating woman and, at least at the moment of the ending, to insist upon her domestication. However, these revisions were neither particularly substantial nor systematic. Both the heroine's final sacrifice and her punishment remain anomalies, at odds with the system of repetition which governs the progression of the narrative as a whole. It is only through a series of singularly abrupt reversals—Lily's change of heart, the failure of Trenholm's suicide attempt—that the formation of the couple becomes possible.

Baby Face is not an isolated case. Other gold-digger films posed severe problems, given the form of the revisions routinely negotiated by the Studio Relations Committee. Moreover, the compromise that censors reached with the studio in the case of *Baby Face*, in which the heroine was punished at the end, was simply not possible in many of the other films, in which comic form dictated a happy ending. Thus, it became even more difficult for industry censors to negate the image of the calculating, aggressive woman, or reinstate a normative view of the relations between the sexes.

At the conclusion of *Red Headed Woman*, for example, the heroine is rejected by her wealthy husband, who has been reconciled with his virtuous former wife. Town gossips predict the redhead will end "in the gutter," but this punishment does not occur. Instead a tag ending shows her in Paris, in the company of a rich old marquis and a handsome young chauffeur (played by Charles Boyer). The ending of *She Done Him Wrong* is more ambiguous, since the heroine is at least outwardly reformed. Diamond Lil is taken into custody by a detective (played by Cary Grant) during a roundup of the criminals with whom she has been associated. He confiscates the diamonds which other men have given to Lil and replaces them with a diamond engagement ring. The ring thus symbolizes a legitimate relationship, in contrast to her other "illicit" ones. But there is no sense that Lil is at all repentant or remorseful about her past. Further, the film does not make a clear distinction between what Lil does out of love for the detective and what she has been doing for profit throughout the film: she continues to receive diamonds and male protection in exchange for sex. As in *Baby Face*, marriage is the ultimate term in a series of sexual exchanges.

Unlike *Red Headed Woman* or *She Done Him Wrong*, *Bed of Roses* lays much greater emphasis upon the heroine's reformation. Nonetheless, the film never entirely renounces the gold-digger's credo. Having fallen in love, Lorry gives up her penthouse and jewels and, feeling remorseful and unworthy of her true love, goes to live alone and work in a department store. Her best friend, Minnie, eventually provides a happy resolution to the romance by reuniting the couple. The last shot of the film centers on Minnie, who has inherited Lorry's diamond brace-let, and presumably her wealthy protector. She kisses the stones and announces, "I love happy endings." *The Greeks Had a Word for Them* ends with a similar bifurcation between the romantic lead and the sec-ondary characters. Jean, one of the gold diggers, is about to enlarge her collection of jewels by marrying a dignified old gentleman. However, she gets drunk on champagne with her two friends, Polaire and Schatzy, and becomes nostalgic for the gay life. The girls abscond with the jewels, taking a boat to Paris in the company of two handsome aviators. At the MPPDA's advice, one of the three is married off at the end: Polaire's former beau appears on board ship and they are reconciled.[49] As in most of these films, then, a "legitimate" couple is formed. But at the same time, the materialism of the gold-digger's credo remains triumphant, if only at the level of secondary characters. Moreover, the ending retains a pre-dominantly cynical tone, the image of the exploitative woman distinctly at odds with the romantic or sentimental posture typical of the classical happy end.

Because of their endings, the gold-digger films were quite difficult to justify under the Code. In the case of *Red Headed Woman* and *She Done Him Wrong*, in which comic elements were most pronounced, industry censors had hopes that the comedy itself would offset the potentially offensive aspects of the characterization of the gold digger. Writing to Carl Milliken, an MPPDA official in the New York office, Joy explains how he was led to pass *Red Headed Woman:*

> In the cold projection room it seemed to be entirely contrary to the Code and one which, even though it conformed to the Code, would get us into all sorts of trouble. However, when seeing it with an audience it took on an entirely different flavor. So farcical did it seem that I was convinced that it was not contrary to the Code and would not (if properly advertised) cause us any undue concern.[50]

In the case of *She Done Him Wrong*, James Wingate seems to have adopted a position similar to Jason Joy's. Wingate explains his strategy for dealing with the film to Hays:

> In view of the rather low tone of both the background and characters presented, [we have suggested] that the whole picture be directed and played with sufficient emphasis on the comedy values, and

exaggeration of the manners and customs of the period, [so] as to remove it as far as possible from any feeling of sordid realism.[51]

The Studio Relations Committee thus maintained that the character of the gold digger would be interpreted in a different way in the context of farce. Because comedy was not granted the same status as "realist" works, because it was seen as frivolous and amusing, it allowed for the presentation of material which would otherwise be considered indecent or inadmissible under the Code.

While Joy and Wingate's hypothesis about how audiences would interpret these comedies is intuitively plausible, it does not seem to have worked in practice as a strategy for dealing with the state boards or reform groups. Given the difficulties which the studios encountered in distributing these films, it seems to me that one might well argue the reverse of the hypothesis offered by industry censors. Perhaps the gold-digger films were offensive *because* they departed from melodramatic conventions, because they made light of what had traditionally been represented as a profound and pathetic moral dilemma—the innocent's fall from grace. Of course, it is difficult to determine precisely how audiences reacted to these films in the period. But a negative reaction to these sorts of films is suggested in this account of a distributor's problems with Canadian censorship boards in the case of *Red Headed Woman:*

> I do not think this is, as you suggest, a picture that we can laugh through as we did with *The Greeks Had a Word for Them, It's a Wise Child, Uneasy Virtue* and a few more comedies. There is not anything comical, in the minds of our Methodists, in the modest, and fairy-sweet flower of sex grown suddenly to sunflower proportions. . . .[52]

A reaction similar to that described by the distributor is anticipated in the language of the Production Code itself, which states that seduction and what Joseph Breen refers to as "impure love" are "never the proper subject for comedy."[53] One can well imagine that for those spectators still under the sway of nineteenth-century conceptions of the feminine, who cherished the cult of true womanhood as an ideal, the infraction of its tenets could be contemplated only in the most solemn and didactic of tones.

Whatever the motivation for the public's complaints about the gold-digger films, it seems clear that the kinds of revisions routinely negotiated by the Studio Relations Committee were insufficient to protect the industry. Through innuendo, it was possible for films to evade the strictures against the representation of seductions and sexual exchange. Moreover, it was possible to play up the circumstances of the heroine's rise by stylistic means; in *Baby Face* through the use of camera movement, decor, and music. The formation of "legitimate" romantic couples at the endings of films, or even the punishment of the heroine in more melodramatic versions of the story, did not necessarily override the cumulative effect of these repeated references to the heroine's active pursuit of money, furs, and diamonds. The fascination with class rise in these films was thus a powerful destabilizing force, one that continually upset the configuration of sexual difference which censorship sought to reinforce.

4

Something Other than a Sob Story

Unlike other types of the fallen woman film, which are relatively obscure, the maternal melodrama has been the object of extensive critical investigation, largely by feminist theorists. Among other issues, these analysts have called attention to the way in which the films tend to define motherhood in opposition to female sexuality. For example, writing of *Blonde Venus*, Ann Kaplan argues that in the terms of the male fantasy which dominates the film, the eroticized image of Dietrich as spectacle is incompatible with and ultimately displaces the image of the woman as domestic, wife, and mother.[1] Linda Williams notes a similar tension between the sexualized image of the woman and her maternal role in an analysis of *Stella Dallas*.[2] An examination of the process of self-regulation allows us to specify, in more concrete historical detail, the way in which the concept of motherhood informed and delimited the representation of female sexuality.

Perhaps because it remained closer to nineteenth-century genre conventions, the maternal melodrama did not call forth prolonged criticism or complaint in the early thirties. For example, *The Sin of Madelon Claudet* was actually commended by members of the Atlanta Better Films Committee, one of whom writes to the MPPDA that "I am glad to see a picture where a woman pays for her sin."[3] *Rockabye* was also deemed acceptable by women's groups involved in previewing films, on the grounds that it dealt with mother love.[4] I will argue that the emphasis on motherhood in and of itself provided a way of managing or controlling what the MPPDA considered the potentially offensive aspects of female deviance. From the point of view of the Studio Relations Committee, the concept of motherhood had a real strategic value; it provided the cornerstone of a moralizing and highly normative discourse which defined the woman's place in terms of her function within the domestic sphere.

Blonde Venus

Like most of his films, Joseph von Sternberg's *Blonde Venus* is highly eccentric. It is described by its director as a "rigorous excursion into style," a script written to be "something other than the sob stories which were then being submitted."[5] Although it is far from a typical example of the genre, I have chosen to analyze the film because it was a limit case. Subject to severe cuts by the state boards at the time of its release in 1932, it was withdrawn from distribution on Joseph Breen's recommendation after 1934. Precisely because the treatment of motherhood was overdetermined, by censorship, by genre convention, and more broadly by an ideology of the family, it is interesting to examine how this example of the maternal melodrama came to pose problems for the MPPDA and the industry.

Blonde Venus departs from genre conventions and more broadly from the principles of narrative continuity which are usually associated with the Hollywood cinema. Its idiosyncrasies reveal how dependent censorship was on conventional narrative modes—on generic formulas, on the establishment of stable unities of character, and an unambiguous linkage of cause and effect. For it is by manipulating narrative at this level that the film manages to bypass the limitations imposed by self-regulatory policy and procedure.

The story of *Blonde Venus* comprises a strange amalgamation of genre conventions. Elements of the gold-digger plot are superimposed upon the story of a mother threatened with separation from her child: at two distinct points in the film the mother becomes wealthy via men. The film also invokes elements of the Sadie Thompson story. The heroine travels to an exotic locale, in this case the American South, where poverty ultimately forces her into prostitution. The heroine's rise is thus made to alternate with her decline in class.

The story opens with the mother's transgression and expulsion from the family. In the first version of the script, Helen and Ned Faraday live in New York with their son, Johnny (in the film there is an additional sequence, an opening in Germany, in which Ned meets Helen).[6] As part of a bedtime ritual, they enact the story of their meeting for their son. Later that same night, Helen learns that Ned, a chemist, is suffering from exposure to radioactive chemicals. He needs to travel to Germany for treatment but does not have the money to pay for the trip. Helen announces that she will return to the stage, her former profession, in order to help him.

Helen gets a job singing in a nightclub (as the Blonde Venus) and there meets a wealthy "politician," Nick Townsend. She procures money from Nick to send Ned abroad. After her husband's departure, at Nick's request, she quits her job and she and Johnny move into a luxurious apartment which he provides. Two weeks before Ned is due to return home, Helen goes off to a resort with Nick. Ned returns home early, learns of Helen's affair, and angrily demands a separation in which he will have custody of the child.

Helen kidnaps the boy and this initiates the sequences comprising her "fall." With Ned and the police pursuing her, Helen must keep on the road and in disguise. Just outside of Savannah, she tricks one of the detectives who has been following her. She picks him up, goes out for a drink with him and takes him back to her lodging, only then revealing her true identity. At this point, she gives Johnny up to Ned and reaches the nadir of her decline, taking a bed in what the script calls the "Ladies Rockbottom Hotel."

The fall is abruptly reversed but, in contrast to most films within the cycle (e.g., *Baby Face*), her rise is not the focal point of the action. Helen leaves the hotel announcing that she can "find a better bed." In the first version of the script, she goes to Nick to get money to further her career (but this is dropped from the film). After a time lapse she appears, already a success, on the Paris stage. The stereotype of the gold digger is evoked, however, when a character notes in passing that she has "used men like stepping stones." She is again pursued by Nick, and although she says she is through with love, she returns to New York where their engagement is announced. Nick gets permission from Ned for Helen to see Johnny. The boy requests that his parents repeat the bedtime ritual given in the opening sequence. In the course of the repetition, the Faradays are reconciled.

The process of negotiation was complicated in this instance by a dispute which Lamar Trotti, an industry censor, describes between "Von Sternberg and Marlene Dietrich on one side and the studio officials on the other."[7] The Studio Relations Committee negotiated with B. P. Schulberg, the producer, on the three successive drafts of the screenplay, which had been the subject of prior negotiations between the director and the studio. Censors found the first draft of the script, written by Sternberg, "utterly impossible." But they did not comment on this draft as the producer was already planning to ask for drastic revisions.[8] Trotti found the second version, prepared according to B. P. Schulberg's specifications, better than the first, but still problematic.[9] When Sternberg and Schulberg were reconciled, a third version was prepared which reinstated much of the director's original material.[10] In some respects, however, particularly the ending, the Studio Relations Committee considered the third draft an improvement upon the studio's version.[11] It should be emphasized that industry censors were not entirely aligned with either the director or the producer. And this three-way process of negotiation made censorship even more difficult. Trotti notes that "the studio, having taken a position with Von Sternberg, will fight like the devil against our suggestions."[12] Thus, most of the changes in scripts in this case were not made expressly at the behest of the Studio Relations Committee or for purposes of censorship. Still, it is possible to get a sense of what censors disapproved of in the successive versions and what, in their view, was necessary to render the final film acceptable to the boards.

Blonde Venus leads us to consider the disparity between the Studio Relation Committee's strategy for dealing with detail and its strategy for dealing with narrative considered as a whole. At a global level, censorship clearly sought to encourage didactic, that is, unambiguous, forms of representation. The Studio Relations Committee wanted to be able to establish a unified moral which could be ascribed to a film in its entirety. At the level of detail, however, the process of negotiation between producers and industry censors frequently resulted in the indirect representation of ideas or events deemed potentially offensive. In the instance of *Blonde Venus* these two levels of censorship were at odds with one another. The director demonstrated a decided proclivity for indirect modes of representation, and in particular for highly elliptical presentations of the action, which was largely complicit with the Studio Relations Committee's strategy for dealing with offensive detail. I will argue, however, that this mode of narration engendered ambiguities at a more global narrative level that worked against the interests of censorship.

According to censors, there were three basic problems with this story. The Studio Relations Committee warned that Helen's affair with Nick, which is present in all three versions of the script, was likely to be cut by the boards.[13] In the correspondence there is much less discussion of the sequences in which Helen resorts to prostitution.[14] Nonetheless, these were censored. A comparison of the three scripts reveals the gradual elimination, or "softening," of scenes in which Helen is shown in the act of soliciting. Finally, there is a very brief memo in the case file which indicates that Harold Hurley of the Paramount legal department was worried because Helen works in a Harlem nightclub, and performs for blacks. The memo states, "Mr. Hurley seems to share our [the Studio Relations Committee's] feeling that this would be questionable, especially in Southern States where such equality is frowned upon."[15] There are several references to blacks, as well as a reference to Harlem, which are eliminated in the second and third versions of the script.[16]

I want to concentrate on the treatment of the adulterous love affair because this seems to have been the central point of negotiation for the Studio Relations Committee and because its position is most clearly documented in this instance. In general, the studio's version of the affair was the least offensive at the level of *content* (for example, Helen does not move into Nick's apartment). However, the studio's script adopts what is by far the most explicit *mode of representation*. Both Sternberg's first and third drafts elide scenes present in the studio's version, and there is relatively less dialogue spelling out the intentions and feelings of the principal characters. The revisions which the Studio Relations Committee asked for in the final draft of the script exacerbated both of these tendencies, so that, in the completed film, the use of ellipsis has been extended and the reliance upon dialogue further diminished. Thus, while industry censors were never very happy with Sternberg's plot, their recommendations for dealing with the problem of adultery jibe with his predilection for elliptical or indirect modes of representation.

Consider, for purposes of contrast, Sternberg's third draft and the studio's treatment of the love affair. In the studio's version, Helen and Nick meet in the nightclub and he asks her out. In the next scene, in Nick's apartment, he leads her to admit that she is married and needs money for the sake of her husband. He then gives her the money and sends her home. The dialogue makes it clear that at this point, Helen is interested only in saving Ned and that Nick, while desiring Helen, does not act on this. After Ned's departure, Nick escorts Helen and Johnny to a restaurant, where he gives her money so that she can quit her job. The next scene is situated some time after Ned's departure. Helen announces Ned is cured and will come home. Nick declares his love, asking her to go away to the resort, and she assents. Thus, there is a clear progression from the night of their first encounter in which Helen takes only money, to the trip to the resort in which Helen has become Nick's mistress.

There are some differences in plot between the second and third versions of the script. Most notably, Helen must sleep with Nick at their first encounter in order to procure the money. But while the plot could be considered "more offensive," it is told in an indirect manner which was ultimately congenial with the strategies of censorship. Consider the scene in which Helen is persuaded to give up her job following Ned's departure. In the studio's version of the script, Nick meets Helen at the dock and takes her out. He then gives her money and convinces her to leave the club. Sternberg's version elides this encounter. The meeting at the dock is followed by a telephone conversation between O'Connor, the manager of the nightclub, and Nick. Nick announces that Helen has quit work. His subsequent conversation with Helen indicates that he will support her. But, in contrast to the studio's draft, money does not actually change hands, and the moment of decision, in which Helen consents to Nick's proposition, remains implicit. Similarly, Helen's decision to move into a flat provided by Nick is not shown directly. He suggests the move in one scene, and in the next she returns to her old flat, now empty, to pick up the mail. Thus, Sternberg's script elides scenes in which Helen acts upon Nick's suggestions, in favor of those which are at the periphery of this action (Nick's telephone call, Helen's retrieval of her mail).

This use of ellipsis is very different from that in *Baby Face*, for example. It is a question not of removing explicit references to the sex act, but of shifting emphasis away from major turning points in the plot. Nonetheless, it was congenial with the aims of censorship since it alleviated the necessity of scenes likely to be regarded as problematic— Helen taking money from Nick, moving into his apartment. This coincidence between Sternberg's technique and the interests of the Studio Relations Committee becomes most evident in their review of the third version of the script. Censors call for revisions which, in effect, intensify the tendencies already apparent there.

In reviewing the third draft of the script, censors complain about scenes in which potentially offensive actions are made explicit and, as in the case of *The Easiest Way*, advocate the ambiguous treatment of the illicit love affair. Joy writes that he is "very much perturbed about the situation in which Helen deliberately accept Nick's invitation to go away for two weeks and to a less extent about the prostitution of herself and frank confession of the fact to her husband," and he concludes, "I don't know how you can tell that part of the story without getting into trouble."[17] In the same letter, Joy points to three specific scenes, two of which have been altered in the final release print. First, in the scene after her performance, Joy complains that "the audience is informed that Helen will stay with Nick," that is, sleep with him for money. Second, censors complain about the dialogue in the scene in which Nick persuades Helen to go away with him. Finally (and this is the one scene that is not altered), the confrontation between Helen and Ned, in Joy's view, seems "to state the facts [of the affair] too deliberately."

In response to these comments, the final release print has been made even more elliptical than the third version of the script. The scene in which Helen goes to Nick's apartment after their first meeting is eliminated, an elision which renders the acquisition of the money unmotivated, almost illogical. After the show, Nick meets Helen in her dressing room. She turns down his offer of a date. The offer of a bracelet is also refused. Helen says: "I don't accept bracelets from strangers." Nick replies, "There is no reason why we should remain strangers," and writes a check. Although Dietrich plays this scene in a rather flirtatious way, Nick is not actually promised anything in dialogue. And, given that she does not even agree to go out with him, his motivation in giving her the check is unclear. This lack of clarity serves the purposes of censorship in so far as it softens or obscures the idea of exchange.

In the scene in which Nick invites Helen to go away with him, censors object to lines of dialogue which clarify the status of Helen's liaison. Joy complains, "she [Helen] explains why she came to him [Nick] in the first place. Because she needed the money—which defines the affair definitely as prostitution. Then she indicates that the affair has been continued because she cared for him and explains how some women can love two men at once without feeling any guilt. . . . All of this scene as it is now written . . . forecasts trouble."[18] The final release print eliminates the line in which Helen says she originally went with Nick for his money and also the line about her being in love with two men at once. In accommodating the Studio Relations Committee here, Sternberg pushes further in the direction of deemphasizing major turning points in the action. Nick proposes that they go away together, and the following scenes—of Ned's arrival in New York and return to an empty flat—indicate Helen's assent. But, unlike both the second and third versions of the script, the change in her attitude to Nick is not explicitly marked in dialogue.

My discussion has focused on the treatment of the love affair because the Studio Relations Committee's negotiating stance is clearest at this point. However, the treatment of the sequences concerning Helen's descent into prostitution seem to follow along similar lines. In the process of revision, the scenes in which she solicits men are either amended or elided, and dialogue which labels her a prostitute is changed. For example, in the first version of the script, Helen is arrested on the street by an undercover cop, and in the next scene she appears in court, on trial for soliciting.[19] By the final release print, the scene of Helen on the streets has been removed; she appears in court without any arrest to motivate her trial. Further, the charge has been changed from "soliciting" to "vagrancy." This kind of construction is both typical of Studio Relations Committee policy, which aims for the elimination of material explicitly identifying the fallen woman's status, and typical of Sternberg, who often leaves implicit scenes which are crucial for the motivation of the action.

The complicity between Sternberg and the Studio Relations Committee seems to extend beyond the treatment of detail to the ending of *Blonde Venus*. Joy and Trotti were aligned with Sternberg, and against Schulberg, in the prolonged debate on the final scene. From the point of view of the Studio Relations Committee, the studio's ending violated the rule of compensating moral values. The ending of the studio's draft of the script pairs off Helen and Nick rather than Helen and Ned. Upon Helen's return from Paris, Nick reveals that Ned has been having an affair with his housekeeper. He threatens to expose this sordid affair in the course of a trial for custody of Johnny. Ned then abandons the boy to his mother, and Helen and Nick make plans to marry. Although the studio's plot is more convoluted than that of the film, it seems to me to be motivated in a more compelling way at the level of character. I surmise that the studio found Ned's harshness toward his wife unsympathetic, as have more recent critics,[20] and therefore sought to reconstitute the couple around the more agreeable romantic lead. Another effect of the studio ending is that Helen remains a success as "star" and as wife of a millionaire. The film is thus made to conform to the general trajectory of class rise which was both conventional and highly popular in this period.

Industry censors, however, object vociferously to the studio's ending. Lamar Trotti writes:

> It does not seem proper to have that [Helen's] affair justified in the minds of the audience by tearing down the character of the husband, who, up to this point, has been a decent man who was deceived by his wife.[21]

Trotti complains about the way in which the studio's version undermines Ned, a character who, for him, represents a moral position or point of view. This kind of reasoning is typical of the Studio Relations Committee. According to the rule of compensating moral values, censors generally advocated the final punishment and suffering of "bad" characters or their regeneration. The problem with the studio's ending of *Blonde Venus*, then, for Trotti, is that the compensatory logic has gone askew. One act of adultery is balanced off, "justified," by one still worse. That is, Helen's affair, which is motivated at the beginning of the film in terms of financial need, as a sacrifice to save her ailing husband, is made to look good in relation to Ned's illicit liaison.

I think it can be argued that Sternberg's ending goes further than the studio's in undermining or destabilizing the domestic ideal. The studio advocated the formation of the romantic couple, a highly conventionalized means of achieving narrative closure within the classical cinema. And building upon this logic, censors sought to superimpose a moral upon the moment of resolution—the couple formed must be the "legitimate" one, purged of the taint of adultery through the narrative logic of punishment and redemption. The sophisticated and wickedly perverse irony of Sternberg's rendering of the ending becomes apparent if we situate it between the Scylla and Charybdis of the studio's "happy ending" and the censor's tale of maternal sacrifice and regeneration. Sternberg's ending destabilizes the romantic idea of courtship which is the precondition of *both* the studio's *and* the censor's preferred ending.

The director's insistence on pairing Helen and Ned for the ending can be explained in terms of a change he made in the third draft of the script (a difference between the first and third versions). Walking with his comrades in a forest, Ned encounters Helen, with a group of actresses, bathing in a pool. This event is retold, in the form of a bedtime story for the child, Johnny, near the opening of the film. The story is repeated yet again, at the boy's insistence, when Helen returns home, and it constitutes the primary device by which husband and wife are reconciled. Thus, the director's choice for the ending is consistent with the establishment of a pattern of repetition.

It is usually argued that repetition works at various levels within the classical text to reduce ambiguity and promote closure.[22] However, in this instance, repetition undermines the formation of the couple and renders the ending highly ambiguous. This effect is due to the contrast between the first and last scenes. In the opening sequence, Ned watches Helen and her comrades swimming. He "lives out" his fascination for Helen, as it were, in the highly voyeuristic shots of the women's bodies. In contrast, in the final sequence, Ned frequently turns his gaze away from his wife as she stands beside the boy's crib. He appears disenchanted with the story of their first encounter and must be persuaded to play his part for Johnny. The contrast between these scenes is heightened through the motif of performance. The very fact that the reiteration of the story of falling in love is presented as a fairy tale for Johnny underscores, precisely, its status as fiction. Thus, while the repetition establishes a parallel between the beginning and the ending, the *differences* between the scenes are so marked that the final reconciliation has a hollow and rather dissonant quality and the expectation of closure is not entirely fulfilled.

It seems unlikely that industry censors would have registered the rather subtle discordances which belie the narrative closure in *Blonde Venus*. In any case, their preference for Sternberg's ending follows, not from the representation of the couple, but from the way the ending, and more generally the film as a whole, deals with Helen as mother. I infer this on the basis of two letters written by Jason Joy.[23] As was routine in cases in which he anticipated problems with external censorship boards, Joy prepared a statement for studio personnel explaining why he considered the film acceptable (studio personnel could then mount a campaign to get the film past the state censor boards with a minimum of cuts). The letters cover every point in the plot which might plausibly have been found offensive—not only adultery but the idea of prostitution which is suggested at several points in the film. This material is defended in terms of the moral logic which Joy ascribes to the narrative in toto: Helen remains a loyal mother, she suffers for her adulterous love affair and undergoes a moral regeneration. Thus, while she seems to enter upon a life of prostitution, this is only to provide for her son.

Further, she gives up custody of her child when she realizes she cannot care for him, "thereby sacrificing her own happiness for his good." And, although she becomes rich in Paris, she is not happy there and gives up her luxurious life, "to return to her husband and child on the same economic level which she had left. . . ."[24]

The strategy of Joy's reading, then, is to recuperate Helen's adultery and her deviations from the maternal role in terms of her "underlying" motives and desires as a mother. This is a very powerful logic, since even the worst transgressions can be made to reinforce the woman's position within the family. No matter how far she appears to stray, the fallen woman never really leaves home.

The logic which governed Joy's reading was not invented by him, and was certainly not limited to *Blonde Venus*. Censorship is aligned with a convention well established within the maternal melodrama. In *The Sin of Madelon Claudet*, the heroine embarks upon a career as a courtesan in order to support her son. In *Confession*, a cabaret singer with a shady past commits murder, apparently out of sexual jealousy; but we discover, through a series of flashbacks at her trial, that she has done so in order to prevent her daughter's seduction by the man who caused her own downfall. In *The House on 56th Street* the heroine agrees to work in a gambling joint, under the control of a mobster, in order to buy his silence for a murder committed by her daughter.[25] Even in the films about gold diggers one can find traces of this kind of separation between motive and action. Lily's coldness and avariciousness in *Baby Face* are justified, to some degree, by what we know of her motive—to gain control of her life and escape prostitution at the hands of the men in the steel town.

Sternberg's handling of genre conventions is far from typical, however, and I would argue that *Blonde Venus* deviates from the general impetus to sanctify the heroine's transgressions by her motives and status as a mother. In this sense, *Blonde Venus* defies the strategy of Joy's reading.

In justifying this film to the boards, Jason Joy emphasized the disjuncture between motive and action—Helen's actions were rendered inoffensive, he argued, because at the level of intention she remained a loyal wife and mother. But the disjuncture between motive and action is pushed to peculiar extremes in the case of this film. Helen's "good" intentions are made incongruous with the postures she assumes. Most important, Helen proves her devotion to her son by kidnapping him and taking to the streets. The maternal is thereby severed from its usual connection with the domestic sphere, as the film emphasizes the moth-

er's status as outlaw/prostitute. This process is summed up in a particularly striking dissolve which connects the image of mother and child
with the police file in which she is labeled as outlaw (see Figure 4.1). A
scene in which she feeds and cares for Johnny in a cafe leads to a bargain
with the fat, leering owner of the restaurant. While the dialogue here
states only that she will wash dishes for the meal, the idea of a tawdry
sexual exchange is unmistakably conveyed through the actor's performance and the final shot of the scene, a low-angle shot which emphasizes
his cigar, upright in his mouth (see Figure 4.2). In another sequence,
Helen approaches the detective who has been pursuing her and Johnny.
She accosts him on the street and accompanies him to a bar, where she
is shown drinking beer and flirting rather outrageously (see Figures 2.4,
2.5, and 4.3). At the same time, without revealing her identity, she
engages in an argument concerning the woman he is pursuing, thus
defending her own actions in terms of mother love. The point is that the
concept of the maternal is consistently aligned with female deviance.

The mise-en-scène of the ending also destabilizes the equation between the maternal and the domestic. The film does not evoke the image

4.1

4.2

4.3

of the streetwalker here, but rather that of the glamorous star. Helen returns from Paris wearing a sequin-trimmed coat which is out of keeping with Faraday's dirty and cramped apartment (see Figure 4.4). She takes off her coat to give Johnny a bath, only to reveal a long-sleeved, backless evening gown which is even more inappropriate for this task (see Figure 4.5). Thus, through the visuals, Helen comes to seem out of place within the space of the family, her domestic role hovering on the absurd.

Through visual style, then, *Blonde Venus* exploits the incongruity between Helen's image as streetwalker or star and her domestic role as mother. The heroine's devotion to her son is represented in ways which disturb the affiliation between motherhood and domesticity, the very ideal which made motherhood of primary "moral" and strategic value for the Studio Relations Committee.

Jason Joy's defense of the film also depends upon a reading of Helen's interior states, her "real" maternal feelings. Frequently, however, the film is quite difficult to interpret at this level. In part because of its highly elliptical mode of narration, *Blonde Venus* often obscures Helen's aims and motives. For example, in Paris Helen tells Nick she does not want to return to New York. She announces she is through with

4.4

4.5

men and even speaks disparagingly of mother love. This stance is abruptly reversed in the following scene, in which a newspaper article relates that Helen and Nick are engaged and have embarked for New York. The break in continuity and the impersonality of the newspaper account deemphasize the character's interior state just when the story hinges upon the question of the heroine's sentiments (or lack thereof). One might assume that Helen returns out of longing for her family, but equally, that she is in love with Nick. Thus, the use of ellipsis, while approved by censors as a means of obfuscating the details of adultery, also makes it difficult to specify Helen's relation to Ned and Johnny. Ambiguity, at this level, works against the aims of censorship by making it difficult to establish a stable motivation for the heroine's action.

There are a number of other instances in which the motivation of the action in *Blonde Venus* makes it difficult to interpret Helen's "real" intentions. I want to concentrate on one segment which was of particular concern to the Studio Relations Committee: Sternberg's treatment of the adulterous love affair. Despite the fact that this segment was very heavily censored at the level of detail, it remains one of the most excessive and scandalous portions of the film, even, I think, for present-day audiences.

The way in which the film bypasses censorship becomes clear if we consider how Helen's first nightclub performance, "Hot Voodoo," inflects the spectator's understanding of the development of the love affair between Helen and Nick. The affair with Nick is doubly motivated, once at the level of narrative in that he can resolve the problem of Ned's poverty and illness, and a second time at the level of spectacle in that he is photographed as the most important spectator for the performance of Hot Voodoo, an event which initiates the affair as such. The question, then, is how this spectacle functions as motivation, and explanation, for the subsequent development of the action.[26]

The "Hot Voodoo" number verges on self-parody through the sheer weight of accumulated metaphor. Consider the refrain and lyrics of the first verse:

> Did you ever happen to hear a Voodoo
> Hear it, and you won't give a damn what you do.
> Tom-toms put me under a sort of hoo-doo
> And the whole night long
> I don't know the right from the wrong.
> Hot Voodoo—black as mud
> Hot Voodoo—in my blood
> It carries me back to a cannibal isle.
> Hot Voodoo—dance of sin
> Hot Voodoo—worse than gin
> I want to start dancing in cannibal style.
> That beat gives me a wicked sensation
> My conscience wants to take a vacation.
> Got Voodoo—head to toes
> Hot Voodoo—burn my clothes.
> I want to start dancing
> Just wearing a smile!

Sexuality is constructed as exotic, allied with "cannibals," the jungle, voodoo. In performance, this set of associations is accentuated by the costumes—the chorus wears body-length primitive masks—and the music, which is decidedly percussive. Dietrich, who first appears in a gorilla suit, is thereby associated with the primitive, at the center of a symbolic constellation which links female sexuality, animals, and blacks.

For several reasons, the connection between the spectacle and narrative—the melodrama of the couple—is not immediate. First, the performance introduces a certain floating of identity. In taking the job, Helen disguises her connection to Ned and Johnny. Helen's agent changes her name from Faraday to Jones, and this designation, a state of virtual anonymity, gives way to another devised by the club manager for the purposes of the act: the Blonde Venus. Also, the extreme stylization of her costume—for example, she wears a tall wig pierced by an arrow— heightens the motif of disguise. Along with the assumption of a persona indicated within the diegesis, there is also a play upon the persona of the star. This becomes apparent if we consider the various stages of her appearance in the opening segments of the film. Dietrich's appearance in New York as Ned's wife runs counter to the style of the opening and more generally the conventions of "glamour" photography. The space of the apartment is dark and confined. Dietrich wears an apron, her hair obscured by a kerchief. While there are some flattering close-ups in this segment, Dietrich tends to be shown in long shot performing a variety of mundane tasks: bathing the baby and putting him to bed (see Figures 4.6

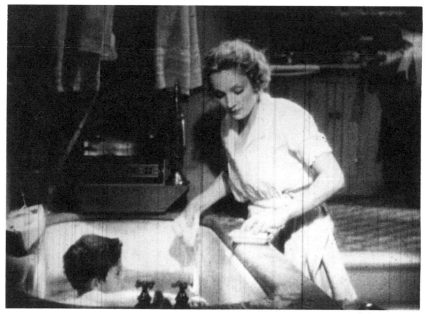

4.6

and 4.7). The "Hot Voodoo" number provides the return, and with a vengeance, of the image of the star, alluring, glamorous (compare Figures 4.8 and 4.9). In a sense, then, it is not Helen but Dietrich who is the Blonde Venus.

The film exploits this division between character and star to introduce material relating to female sexuality which would otherwise have been taboo. The lyrics connect dancing and transgression ("Hot Voodoo—dance of sin") and take exhibition as the accomplishment of desire ("I want to start dancing in cannibal style . . . burn my clothes"). Indeed, the moment in which the Blonde Venus reveals her costume beneath the ape disguise echoes the line about shedding her clothes and points to her active participation in the display. This emphasis upon the dancer's pleasure redoubles, and is reinforced by, the return of Dietrich's star image and the spectator's pleasure in the spectacle. Of course, given that this is a performance, the film avoids positing any direct relation between Helen's motives and those we might impute to the "I" of the lyrics. Still, there are hints that Helen returns to the stage for her own reasons, apart from Ned's illness (she tells her husband that she was planning to return to work even before his illness). Further, through the

4.7

4.8 Helen at home

4.9 Helen as Blonde Venus

vehicle of performance, the sexuality that Helen must hold back, that cannot achieve expression in the domestic space, is displaced to the space of the stage and image of the star. The film uses spectacle to destabilize the unity or "identity" of character. By this means, it is possible to suggest a whole range of motivations for Helen's action which lie outside the scenario of wifely sacrifice and devotion.

This destabilization of the unity of character has important consequences for the way in which the initiation of the affair between Nick and Helen can be interpreted. I have noted that in the third version of the script, there is a scene in Nick's apartment in which the spectator is led to understand that Helen sleeps with Nick for three hundred dollars. In response to the warnings of the Studio Relations Committee, this is eliminated from the film. Instead, Nick writes Helen a check at the club, for reasons which are not made explicit in dialogue. However, this exchange is motivated at the level of the performance. Nick is introduced just prior to Venus's entrance on stage, and there are several point-of-view shots in which he watches, and comments on, the act. Thus, the dynamic of the exchange between these two—her invitation, his desire—is established prior to any dialogue between them, through the alternation between the performance and the look of the male character. Advancing the action in this manner confuses the registers of spectacle and narrative. The dance stands in for the scene in the third version of the script in which we are given to understand that Helen offers herself to Nick. In effect, it superimposes upon the impetus for Helen's affair (she needs money for Ned) the transgressive stance of the Blonde Venus ("I don't know the right from the wrong. . . . I'm going to blazes, I want to be bad.").

In *Blonde Venus*, clearly, the censor's "moral" reading of the story stressed the heroine's domestication. Helen, Joy argued, was a "mother and a good woman," and his whole strategy for the defense of the film was to guarantee the latter on the basis of the former. But this strategy presupposed that the film presented an unambiguous rendering of interior states and the unity or coherence of character—a stable identity to which clear-cut motives could be affixed. *Blonde Venus* eluded censorship at both of these levels. Through the use of ellipsis it consistently downplayed the moments of high melodrama, in which the heroine's sentiments or attitude toward her family would be emphasized (e.g., her decision to return home from Paris, but also her decision to betray Ned in the first place). Through the division between character and star, it introduced a motivation for infidelity which would have been unacceptable if directly attributed to Helen. While it did not entirely foreclose the possibility of the reading which Joy offered to the boards, it opened up an alternate path of interpretation, in which the heroine's transgressions were not recuperated as maternal sacrifice.

Blonde Venus is an atypical case, but not a completely aberrant one. I do not want to suggest that it took an auteur—a von Sternberg, or a Lubitsch—to upset the balance of censorship. The idiosyncrasies of a director like Sternberg flourished as much *because of* as *despite* the constraints imposed on representation within the studio system. *Blonde Venus* could go as far as it did in aligning the maternal and the sexually deviant because Sternberg went to great lengths to accommodate the Studio Relations Committee in the treatment of detail. The film is in many ways the logical extension of a system which favored the development of indirect or allusive forms of representation. Clearly, this system placed industry censors in a highly tenuous position: they were perpetually winning battles and losing the war, effectively defending the representation of material the Code ostensibly forbade.

5

The Production Code Administration's
Policies and Procedures

WHILE THE MPPDA did not routinely keep completed films out of distribution, in February of 1935, when public sentiment against the industry was at its height, Joseph Breen was able to persuade the studios to withdraw a number of films already in release.[1] He was also able to prevent the re-release of some films made in the early thirties which he thought likely to be found offensive. Among these was Sternberg's *Blonde Venus*.[2] Clearly, films which had been considered defensible by the Studio Relations Committee were evaluated differently by industry censors in the latter part of the decade. Self-regulatory policy and procedure altered so that it became relatively more difficult to bypass its constraints, and the ways in which it was possible to play out the conventions of the fallen woman film became considerably more circumscribed.

I will account for these changes in the administration of censorship by examining how the MPPDA reacted to mounting public pressure against the film industry in 1933–34. The most important sources of pressure on the industry — i.e., the publicity arising from the Payne Fund Studies and the Catholic Legion of Decency campaign — have been described at length by Jowett and Sklar. Historians have given relatively little attention to the way in which the MPPDA viewed the events of 1933–34, however, or the specific actions which Hays initiated in response to them.

From the point of view of Hays, I would argue, the problem posed by both the Payne Fund and the Legion was essentially one of negative publicity. This publicity escalated to the point of crisis, what one member of Hays's staff dubbed a "state of war."[3] For not only were individual films, such as *Baby Face*, the object of complaint, but also the industry as a whole was subjected to prolonged and highly visible attacks on the part of social scientists and the church.

The Payne Fund Studies played into long-standing concerns on the part of reform groups about the effects of Hollywood on its audience. A brief review of the tenor of the research will suggest why it posed such a threat to the industry. As I have noted, the research sought to provide a theory and description of how various segments of the population—children, delinquents, immigrant youths—reacted as spectators. At issue were modes of identification specific to them: film's capacity to inspire ideas and emotions.[4] In his summary of the research, Werrett Wallace Charters, the director of the project, argued that the cinema had the capacity to undermine social norms as yet imperfectly interiorized by children and other groups defined as potentially deviant.[5] He argued the cinema could reinforce a tendency to deviancy among these groups, through an appeal to fantasy or emotion, broadly defined.

The claims advanced by the Payne Fund Studies were circulated, and somewhat sensationalized, in popular books and magazines. The research thus focused national attention on issues which previously had been of concern only to relatively marginal groups such as civic and women's organizations. Henry James Forman's *Our Movie Made Children*, a summary written for the general public, appeared in March, before many of the original monographs were published. *McCall's, The Saturday Review of Literature*, and *Parent's Magazine* all published related material.[6] The *Christian Century*, a nondenominational journal which vigorously advocated federal censorship of the movies throughout the thirties, published a series of seven articles which renewed the demand for censorship in light of the research.[7]

Will Hays appears to have been actively concerned with the publicity generated by the Payne Fund Studies. For the years of 1933 and 1934, his papers contain regular reports of pamphlets, newspaper articles, even sermons, which make reference to the Payne Fund research.[8] Soon after the publication of Forman's *Our Movie Made Children*, one MPPDA report suggested that the studies would be used to further the cause of the reform forces: "as long as they go unchallenged, the 'Payneful' charges become accepted as the truth for propagandists for [government] censorship."[9] But perhaps the clearest indication of Hays's concern is that the MPPDA went so far as to sponsor a rebuttal to the Payne Fund "charges," Raymond Moley's *Are We Movie Made?*[10]

At the same time that this crisis was developing in the area of public relations, it was becoming increasingly obvious that the Studio Relations Committee's policies and procedures were not providing adequate protection for the industry. Hays's correspondence registers several complaints about Wingate's performance and Studio Relations Committee policy from sources *internal* to the MPPDA. One of the earliest comments about Wingate's administration derives from Martin Quigley, one of the original authors of the Code. Breen, in a letter to Hays, notes that Quigley was dissatisfied with Wingate's interpretation of policy and application of the Code:

> Q[uigley] has been making the round of the studios hereabouts for the past fortnight. I take it that his plan has been to spend a day in and about each of the studios, chatting with any number of the executives. . . . He feels that the staff which succeeds Col. Joy is not a good one. He tells me that he has this impression, first, from his observation of the working of this group, and, secondly, from some comments which he picked up around the studios. Q[uigley] is terribly disappointed. . . . I never saw him so down in the mouth about anything as he is about the Code.[11]

Quigley's was not the only complaint about the administration of censorship. Another very interesting discussion of the difficulties of Wingate's administration was submitted by one of Hays's West Coast public relations staff, Alice Ames Winter. She notes that Wingate concentrates on potentially censorable details to the exclusion of what she calls the "general flavor" of films.

> It is almost impossible to get anything over to the producers when the issues already raised (as if they were the main issues) have dealt with a phrase or a triviality. How, for example, can you raise the question of a seduction scene that colors a whole drama even though it is not shown in actuality while the censor is thinking only about the elimination of the word "lousy," and [is] not in the least sensitive to the fact that the audience is compelled to do its own dirty thinking on inferences that it cannot escape.
> So we continue to deal inadequately with the problem of the growing hostility on the part of the public—at least the public that

knows how to organize and to talk. . . . the machinery isn't working as it ought to do for the purposes for which you created it.[12]

Winter's letter points to a mode of censorship which we have seen was *routine* in the case of the fallen woman cycle. It was not simply personal incompetence that led Wingate to pass a scene which implied seduction without showing it "in actuality." The Studio Relations Committee routinely used such allusive methods for getting potentially offensive material past the state boards. Given this, Mrs. Winter's letter suggests that what had been standard industry practice in dealing with the boards began to appear increasingly dangerous in the light of the agitation in the public sphere. For clearly while ellipsis and other means of indirect representation might forestall state intervention in any given case, they did not appease the variety of groups which, under the impetus of the Payne Fund Studies, were concerned about the cumulative effect of filmgoing on the spectator.

In the context of widespread public criticism of the industry and internal criticism of the operations of the Studio Relations Committee, Hays undertook a review of Wingate's administration of the Code. He traveled to the West Coast in April of 1933 and personally reviewed a number of films (among them was *Baby Face* which, from his point of view, must have provided ample proof of the failings of the regulatory mechanism).[13] He then initiated a reorganization of the Studio Relations Committee hierarchy. Apparently at the time of Hays's visit it was decided that Joy, then at Fox, would assume greater responsibilities for the evaluation of scripts.[14] But this arrangement lasted only until December, when the Fox studio requested that Joy devote himself full-time to the studio.[15] Breen was then promoted over Wingate and assumed control of the division in January of 1934.[16]

Breen thus controlled the Studio Relations Committee well before the Catholic Legion of Decency campaign came to a head in June of 1934.[17] This chronology is quite important for my evaluation of the changes that took place in the administration of self-regulation in the mid-thirties. In my view, film historians have overemphasized the role of the Legion of Decency in their explanations of the exercise of censorship.[18] Although Breen was himself associated with the Legion of Decency, his administration had to do more than simply respond to this pressure group. We can presume that he was promoted because Hays found Wingate's administration of the Code inadequate for the protection of the industry. Further, he came to power in a social context—the "state of war"—which necessitated a reformulation of industry policy and procedures.

While the Legion was not solely responsible for the changes in the administration of censorship which took place in this period, it certainly helped to strengthen Breen's bargaining position vis-à-vis the studios. It has even been suggested that Breen knowingly used the Legion toward this end. While Breen orchestrated the MPPDA's response to the Legion—there are references to him negotiating with the church hierarchy[19]—there is also some evidence that Breen actively promoted the *formation* of the Legion. In his book on the Production Code Administration, Jack Vizzard claims that Breen, in tandem with Martin Quigley, conspired to have the idea of the organization proposed to the Bishops Convention.[20] I think it likely that the Legion was, if not inspired, then at least fed information by Breen and Quigley.[21] For the Legion was the only reform group of the period that was cognizant of the criticisms of the Studio Relations Committee that were being made within the MPPDA. In public pronouncements, the Legion called attention to the industry's "failure" to abide by the terms of the Production Code,[22] and it consistently demanded more effective regulation at the point of production.

It is not certain that Breen intended to play the Legion off against the MPPDA, but it is clear that, in effect, the pressure exerted by the Legion improved his position within the industry. In June of 1934, at the peak of the Legion campaign, the MPPDA announced a number of changes in the administration of censorship. The Studio Relations Committee was renamed the Production Code Administration. Breen expanded his staff, and thus industry censors could spend more time reviewing the day-to-day process of production.[23] The Production Code Administration also began to review literary properties before they were purchased by the studios.[24] Thus, throughout the decade, Breen could block the acquisition of certain novels and plays. Another of the concessions made by the industry to the Legion was the elimination of the so-called Hollywood Jury,[25] and this is usually said to have given Breen the power to "enforce" the Code. I see this kind of language largely as a function of publicity. Even after this point, Breen continued to negotiate with the studios. The escalating power of the Production Code Administration is most evident in the reformulation of policy, especially in Breen's reinterpretation of the Code, and the kinds of revisions that were routinely made in films and scripts.

The change in self-regulatory policy is rather subtle, for there were many points of continuity between the two administrations. Although the state boards were no longer the primary focus of censorship, the Production Code Administration continued the Studio Relations Committee's practice of warning the studios about details of action or dialogue likely to be cut by the boards.[26] Even in the application of the Code, Breen did not institute radical shifts in policy. For example, the Production Code Administration continued to place emphasis upon the punishment of "bad" characters. But, under Breen, existing policies were elaborated or amended so that it became more difficult for films to elude the constraints of censorship. We can see this in the treatment of both details and narrative in this period.

The Production Code Administration virtually eliminated one of the basic characteristics of the films of the early thirties—the play upon indirect means of representation to avoid cuts by the boards. Consider the treatment of the sex act which, under the Studio Relations Committee, was usually handled by an ellipsis. Breen wrote, in a letter to Hays, that such an act might be suggested, but "must not be openly and explicitly established by detailed dialogue or action, particularly not immediately preceding or immediately following the actual transgression."[27] His prose is somewhat confusing here, but Breen seems to assume a case in which the sex act is elided. He refers to what is possible in the scenes which surround the "actual" transgression. These can not allude to the action which has been omitted. Thus, for example, the rape in *The Story of Temple Drake,* in which the scene prior to the ellipsis clearly shows the man advancing upon the woman, would not have been permitted under the redefinition of policy. In general, after 1934 ellipsis in and of itself was no longer seen as an adequate means of defense, and industry censors began to initiate discussion concerning how it operated within a given sequence to suggest certain ideas or actions.

This is not to claim that after 1934 films never managed to figure material such as adultery or seduction, but censorship was relatively more successful in destabilizing the representation of this material. Often it remains possible for the spectator to interpret scenes or sequences in sexual terms, but this interpretation is not confirmed, and is sometimes explicitly denied, through action or dialogue. For example, in *Camille* (MGM, 1937), Marguerite goes to the country with her lover, Armand. The scene of the couple's arrival at the farmhouse, in which

Armand carries her over the threshold, suggests that they spend the night together. However, in the next scene (the next morning), she is shown alone in her bedroom while it is announced that he has taken up a separate residence at an inn. Hence, the film sets up an interpretation in one scene which it denies in a later one.

In negotiations with producers, the Production Code Administration insisted upon revisions which effectively insured this kind of open-ended treatment of potentially offensive sexual material. In particular, Breen seems to have been more careful than the Studio Relations Committee had been to monitor nonverbal aspects of the scene. As we have noted in the case of *Baby Face*, prior to 1934 ideas which were occluded at the level of dialogue or action could be emphasized by visual means. After 1934, censors devote relatively more attention to set design, performance, and what Breen calls "tone" in an attempt to manage suggestive scenes. Breen reports to Hays that the increase in office staff enabled the Production Code Administration to undertake the review of costumes and set construction.[28] He further notes the importance of atmosphere in the evaluation of films: "Low tone alone may render a whole production unacceptable. The location of scenes and the conduct, the demeanor, the attitude of the players enter very much into the question of the flavor of the appeal of the right or wrong presented."[29] An example of the change in routine occurs in the case of *Private Number* (20th Century-Fox, 1936). The heroine's fall is precipitated by a man who takes her to what the script calls a "gambling house" where she is subsequently arrested on a morals charge. Nowhere is the house referred to as a house of prostitution. The point of contention between Breen and Darryl Zanuck, the producer, was the degree to which the script, and by extension the film, could indirectly suggest the nature of the heroine's liaison. Breen objected:

> The house is operated by Grandma Gammon, a lady suggestive of an elderly madam. There is the trim colored maid who looks through a peephole before opening the door, Cokely's winking at the maid, the drinking of champagne in a private parlour and the painting of a voluptuous lady in a harem. All tend, in our judgment, to give this house the color and flavor of a house of ill fame.[30]

Thus, even though through the ruse of the gambling establishment the script avoided mention of the word "prostitution," Breen moved to block the representation of this idea at the level of performance and decor.

After 1934, then, the treatment of potentially offensive action shifted in the direction of greater ambiguity. While seduction, adultery, or illicit sexuality were not forbidden as topics, it became much more difficult to call attention to such ideas even through the nonverbal aspects of the scene. As a result, in many cases such as that of *Camille*, it is difficult for the spectator to pinpoint with certainty when or how the heroine's sexual transgressions occur.

It should be noted that ambiguity in the treatment of detail did not always work in the interests of censorship. The screwball comedies of the late thirties and early forties proved to be a constant source of irritation and complaint for the MPPDA precisely because they were so adept at exploiting the sorts of denial mechanisms typically favored by the Production Code Administration.[31] In a review of the script of *Palm Beach Story*, Breen noted that civic and religious groups "have let it be known that stories centering around the theme of a light treatment of marriage and divorce . . . have been a source of serious complaint."[32] There are letters of complaint on file in the case of *The Lady Eve* and *The Miracle of Morgan's Creek*.[33] *Two-Faced Woman* was condemned by the Legion of Decency upon its release, and one newspaper editor summed up the tenor of the complaints about this, and similar, films:

> For the last half dozen years, Hollywood has been having a high old time honeymooning. I mean, that with a marriage license, however technical and fictitious, anything goes. We have had a succession of sizzling bedroom sequences that are nearly as wanton as if the dalliance were without benefit of clergy . . . I reluctantly agree with the Legion of Decency; marriage in a good many films is represented as a one-woman harem and a knowing, smirky quality has been too evident.[34]

In my view, screwball posed problems for the Production Code Administration insofar as the plots revolved around misinterpretations, around the difficulty of knowing the truth about the heroine's putatively guilty past. In *Bachelor Mother*, for example, the heroine is mistakenly suspected of having given birth to an illegitimate baby. Many of the jokes are predicated upon the disparity between the heroine's (and spectator's) knowledge and that of the other characters—who assume they know who the mother is and concern themselves solely with getting her to reveal the identity of the *father*. The story thus develops "as if" the heroine had had an illegitimate baby, although the film assures us that she "really" did not. Allusions to adultery in the case of *My Favorite Wife* are somewhat more suggestive. The heroine returns to her family after having been shipwrecked and living for seven years on a desert island with an athlete, a magnificent physical specimen. Her husband suspects the worst. The film rather coyly refrains from definitively proving him wrong. *My Favorite Wife* thus differs from *Bachelor Mother*, in which the spectator shares the heroine's knowledge of events and is thereby convinced of her innocence. Both films, however, introduce some level of uncertainty concerning the "fact" of the heroine's transgressions. In this sense, they both utilize the mechanism of denial to introduce notions of sexual deviance which would have otherwise been taboo.

After 1934, then, it was still possible for producers to devise ways of "getting around" the constraints of censorship in order to allude to material deemed offensive. At the same time, however, Breen's application of the Code with regard to the treatment of story and character was relatively more severe than that of the Studio Relations Committee, and more narrowly circumscribed the sorts of options available to producers. Breen took the language of the Code quite seriously. In his annual report to Hays for 1935, he painstakingly annotated each of the sections of the document, interpreting ambiguous clauses and noting how they had been amplified in practice. In correspondence with producers, Breen frequently quoted whole sections of the Code in support of his complaints and suggestions. Through this kind of attention, it became the focal point of the routine of censorship. From the point of view of the Production Code Administration, their primary task was not to anticipate the reaction of censor boards, or even the Catholic Legion of Decency, but to determine if scripts were acceptable under the Code. The whole process of censorship, then, became relatively more centralized than in the early thirties, while industry policy became more rigorously, and rigidly, defined.

In terms of particular applications, one of the biggest differences between Breen's use of the Code and that of his predecessors was the shift in the attitude toward endings. In the annual report of 1936, which is devoted to the Code, Breen noted that stories should not be evaluated solely on their resolution. Concerning the problem of illicit sex he writes: "it is not a satisfactory solution, for example, to have the principals simply and suddenly marry in the final scene after leading an alluring life of sin throughout the play." More generally, he noted the inadequacy of "the subterfuge of attempting to wipe out a protracted wrong by one last line of dialogue affirming the right. Dialogue alone carries no conviction."[35] Breen's stance here seems to have become industry policy. At least, I have not found any cases in the later period comparable to *The Easiest Way* or *Baby Face*, in which a film considered extremely offensive was rendered acceptable to censors almost solely through changes in the ending.

In seeking to attach moral significance to films, Breen utilized many of the same devices that Joy and Wingate had employed. In the annual report for 1936, Breen argued that the narrative as a whole should offset or compensate for the character's transgressions. The methods for doing this were summarized in a list of "compensating moral values" which included: "good characters, the voice of morality, a lesson, regeneration of the transgressor, suffering and punishment."[36] Prior to 1934, the Studio Relations Committee had advocated the use of all of these devices. What distinguishes Breen's administration, then, is that he was in a position to require a relatively more extensive *elaboration* of them. Thus, for example, the heroine's deviations from the familial norm were not only condemned in isolated scenes of denunciation, but condemned more unobtrusively, through the working out of the plot. The Production Code Administration's aim in this regard was to insure the heroine's prolonged condemnation, disgrace, or self-mortification: a dramatic and irrevocable fall. While not all of the fallen woman films produced after 1934 stressed the element of punishment to the degree Breen deemed appropriate, in every case producers had to find a way to work with or around this requirement.

As a result, one of the Production Code Administration's basic strategies for censoring the fallen woman film was to revert to the nineteenth-century convention of the fall. The trajectory of the fall provided a means of extending the moral significance of a story beyond the confines of the ending to the narrative as a whole. The case of *Anna Karenina* demonstrates this pronounced convergence between the policies and procedures of the Production Code Administration and nineteenth-century genre conventions. There were certainly versions of *Anna Karenina* produced prior to 1934; indeed the 1935 version employed the same director and star as the 1927 version, entitled *Love*. But the point is that this archetypical nineteenth-century formulation of the plot was exhumed amidst the debates and pressures of the late thirties, and, in this social context, was adopted by Breen as an ideal way of dealing with the representation of adultery.

Anna Karenina

In the annual report to Hays for 1935, Breen choose to discuss *Anna Karenina* as an example of the application of the Code. He must have regarded it as a case which put his administration in a good light, a success story. It is of interest, then, because it represents an extreme of censorship. The film is one of a series of lavish Garbo vehicles in which MGM resurrected nineteenth-century genre conventions. *Anna Karenina* (1935) was followed by *Camille* (1937). *Conquest* (1938) did not derive from a nineteenth-century source, but it was set in the nineteenth century, in Napoleon's court, and activates many of the same conventions. From their general outline one can see why these stories would be at least marginally acceptable to Breen. In all of them, the heroine is seduced and more or less unwillingly abandoned, so that the emphasis is upon her unhappy fate. Further, with the exception of the opening scenes of *Camille*, class rise or the exploitation of men by women is not an issue.

The adaptation of *Anna Karenina* opens with Vronsky's visit to Moscow from St. Petersburg where he is in military service. He meets an old friend, Steva, and by coincidence both men are going to the railway station. Vronsky, who goes to meet his mother at the station, is introduced to Steva's sister Anna.

At Steva's request, Anna manages to reconcile her brother, a notorious womanizer, with his estranged wife, Dolly. She also talks with Kitty, a young friend of the family, about her expectations of marriage. The staid Levin has proposed, but Kitty admits she finds Vronsky more attractive. At a ball prior to Anna's departure, Kitty is disappointed when Vronsky actively pursues Anna.

In St. Petersburg, Anna publicly receives Vronsky's attentions. This continues despite warnings which Vronsky receives from the head of his regiment, and Anna, from her husband, Karenin. Vronsky attempts to persuade Anna to leave her husband, but she hesitates out of devotion to her son, Sergei. However, after a month of enforced separation, she decides that she can no longer live with her husband and agrees to accompany Vronsky to Italy.

Upon their return to Russia, relations between the lovers become strained. Anna misses her son. Vronsky, bored, admits that he misses military life. Attempting to create some kind of social life for them, Anna insists that they attend the opera, but there she is snubbed and made an object of gossip. At the same time, Vronsky's mother introduces him to the young and attractive Princess Serokina, hoping to arrange an advantageous marriage.

War is declared and Vronsky announces his intention to reenlist. The lovers argue and Vronsky departs abruptly. Anna follows him to Moscow, hoping to effect a reconciliation. She arrives at the train station just as he is about to leave for the front. She watches from a distance as he bids good-bye to his mother and Princess Serokina. Remaining in the station after Vronsky's departure, Anna commits suicide by jumping before an oncoming train.

Breen seems to have been pleased with even the first version of the script, writing to Louis B. Mayer that he "read with real pleasure your impressive script of *Anna Karenina*. It is indeed a splendid treatment of an originally powerful story."[37] In subsequent negotiations with David Selznick, who was in charge of this production, there were disputes over scenes which showed Anna and Vronsky kissing, and some of this action was eliminated. On the whole, however, the story was little changed. The film was well received upon its release, with Garbo nominated for an Academy Award. The only complaint seems to have come from a small minority within the Catholic Legion of Decency. Members of the Chicago chapter gave the film a "C" rating—"unfit for anybody to see."[38] Upon Breen's request, the bishop of Los Angeles nominated a "jury" of four local priests who viewed this film, among others, and found it "thoroughly and completely acceptable under the provisions of our Production Code."[39] Perhaps this dispute with the Legion motivated Breen to discuss the case in detail for Hays in the annual report for 1935. In any event, his discussion centers upon how the film was evaluated under the Code, and why the treatment of adultery was deemed permissible.

It is a measure of the shift in the whole system of negotiation between producers and censors that Breen writes as if the treatment of the details of the love affair were no longer a problem. He merely notes in passing that adultery is not made explicit in the film: "There is no sensuous dialogue, there is very little physical contact between the principals and there are no bedroom scenes."[40] But this is an important point, for *Anna Karenina* can be seen as a model of the kind of ambiguous treatment of sexual material which became commonplace in the late thirties. Take, for example, the moment of the initiation of the affair. Anna, who has previously resisted Vronsky's advances, agrees to see him alone. Later that evening, Karenin waits for Anna to return home. A brief scene follows between Anna and Vronsky in which she discloses her affection. One might infer that a sexual relation has been established, because of the sudden change in Anna's attitude, and because she has obviously chosen to remain with Vronsky while her husband expects her. The dialogue can also be interpreted in sexual terms. For example, Anna says, "I know now that there is no hope for me," as if something decisive has happened which has determined the course of their relationship. However, the film provides only minimal clues to the nature of the action which precedes Anna's disclosure.[41] The location of the scene remains obscure. It might take place in Vronsky's flat, but this is not definitely established. And while Garbo is prone at the beginning of the scene, she is in a chair, and fully dressed. Thus, nothing directly leads the spectator to place a sexual interpretation upon events. And even if such an interpretation makes sense in the context of the plot, a contrary reading always remains possible. This use of ambiguity, in which the spectator is not forced to make an inference about the omitted action, is typical of the later phase of censorship.

While Breen does not appear overly concerned with the treatment of details, he writes at length about the difficulty of introducing adultery as a basic theme under the terms of the Production Code. His interpretation of the Code here calls for close attention to the representation of the family, or more precisely, the offending couple. Quoting the Code, he states that adultery must not be justified or made to seem "alluring," and it must not "weaken respect for marriage." He reports to Hays that there is frequently difficulty in complying with the Code provisions on adultery, because the audience tends to sympathize with the perpetrators. Sympathy with such characters may lead the spectator to condone their actions: "Undue sympathy for the sinner is liable by association of ideas and momentum of emotion to lead to sympathy with the sin itself. Moreover, excessive sympathy for the sinner creates antipathy for the good characters whose duty it is to hamper and halt his career. Exaggerated sympathy for the adulterous wife may make us hate the faithful husband."[42]

In his evaluation of *Anna Karenina*, Breen enumerates several elements or "compensating moral values" which serve to offset the effects of sympathy for the principal characters, and reinforce the legitimacy of the marital bond. In some respects, Breen's compensating moral values resemble the kinds of revisions which Joy and Wingate typically recommended prior to 1934. Thus he points to denunciation scenes, in which the heroine is chastised, and emphasizes the unhappy ending. However, Breen's application of the Code can be distinguished from previous administrations by its systematic nature. He is, I think, justified when he writes to Hays that "the impression of [Anna's] wrongfulness is continuous and cumulative and becomes complete at the climax."[43] Censorship is no longer confined to isolated scenes but integrated within the continuity of narrative. Not only the succession of events, but the ordering of scenes, and even the organization of point of view, can be seen to fulfill a strategic function.

Anna Karenina sets up Anna's husband, Karenin, to be a "voice of morality." Karenin delivers two rather lengthy, didactic speeches which, in no uncertain terms, assert the value of monogamy and family life. He refers to "the inviolability of the marriage tie," and warns the heroine that "the family cannot be broken up by the whim or caprice or even the sin of one of the partners in marriage." Yet the audience's position with respect to Karenin's pronouncements is not entirely clear. Breen notes that Karenin is an unsympathetic character since he maintains a "superior air," and is sarcastic and unrelenting toward Anna. All of this, in Breen's view, "detracts from his value as a mouthpiece of morals."[44] But I think one of the most interesting aspects of censorship in this case is that the condemnation of adultery is not limited to any one character, or to isolated didactic speeches. There are several scenes in which this judgment is rendered indirectly, woven into the fabric of the text.

Consider the sequence which follows Anna's return to St. Petersburg. She encounters Vronsky at a garden party. The sequence begins with Anna and Vronsky isolated in the background, playing croquet, while the remainder of the guests are seated in the foreground (see Figure 5.1). A pattern of alternation is established between the conversation of the lovers in the background, where Vronsky pays Anna compliments, and the conversation in the foreground, where various members of the party gossip as they observe the game: "Anna and Vronsky are playing a conversational game." "At this rate, they won't finish until nightfall." "Perhaps that is their intention." In an attempt to avoid being watched, Vronsky hits a ball off into a secluded part of the garden. This initiates a new pattern of alternation between the lovers, hidden from view in a

5.1

gazebo, and the public space of the remainder of the company. In public, the hostess, Lydia, greets Karenin. Hidden from view, Vronsky declares his love for Anna. Lydia proceeds to warn Karenin about Vronsky's attentions to his wife. As these two talk in the foreground, Anna and Vronsky return to their game in the background of the shot (see Figure 5.2).

The function of the "mouthpiece of morals," the interdiction of the love affair, cannot be located in any single character. It is figured through the articulation of vision and space. The members of the party come to constitute a collective "point of view." That is, Karenin and the gossips occupy the foreground, a clearly delineated space from which the croquet game is observed. The lovers become objects of this group's scrutiny and criticism when they are exposed to the look of the characters in the foreground.[45] The effect of the love scene would be quite different given another structure of point of view, if, for example, Anna and Vronsky met in a park, unobserved. By placing the lovers under the eye of society and the disapproving husband, the film insists upon the transgressive nature of their interchange. This disapproval is invoked

5.2

even when the lovers are no longer in the actual purview of the assembled company. For example, their retreat to a secluded area of the garden is juxtaposed with Karenin's entrance and acquisition of knowledge about the affair. Further, the later scene in which Anna and Vronsky finally do meet alone is both preceded and followed by shots of Karenin, awaiting his wife's return home. Thus, in almost every scene concerned with the initiation of the love affair, Anna and Vronsky are exposed to some measure of condemnation. This condemnation is not explicit, i.e., a function of dialogue, but rather implicit in the use of space and point of view.

As with its treatment of the "voice of morality," the Production Code Administration's treatment of the problem of the ending tends toward more systematic, and less overt, strategies of censorship. Breen writes to Hays that the unhappy ending alone does not adequately compensate for sympathy elicited for the heroine. "In elaborating on the question of sin and sympathy the Code says in effect that evil, even though later punished, must not be made so attractive that in the end the condemnation will be forgotten and only the apparent joy of the sin will be remembered."[46] His aim, then, was to find some way of extending the effect of the unhappy ending throughout the course of the film. For this reason, he places great stress upon the prolonged suffering of the heroine. He observes, with a certain degree of sadism, that from the moment of the initiation of the affair, "there is not a single hour of unalloyed bliss for Anna."[47] And his description of the plot highlights Anna's progressive isolation and abandonment.

In accordance with Breen's description, I have already noted the concatenation of unhappy events which occupies the latter half of the story. Initially torn between her lover and her son, Anna is eventually forced to relinquish them both. Moreover, individual scenes are set up to dramatize her suffering. Often events follow a progression from bad to worse. For example, in the scene at the opera, Anna and Vronsky enter their box, eliciting stares and whispers from the other members of the audience. Then a potential rival for Vronsky's affections is introduced. Anna watches from a distance as Vronsky's mother invites him to dine with the Princess Serokina. Anna can no longer move in polite society, but the princess, she is told, is the "hit of the season." Finally, she is publicly insulted by a couple in a neighboring box, and Vronsky is very nearly involved in a duel. Thus the succession of events gradually extends and deepens the process of Anna's humiliation.

Anna's fall is further underscored by various references to fate within the film, which set her up as a "doomed" and tragic figure. Her first meeting with Vronsky, at the train station, is punctuated by the accidental death of a railway worker who is crushed beneath an oncoming car. In a rather heavy-handed fashion, she seems to anticipate her own suicide, telling her brother Steva that the accident is an "evil omen." In a similar vein, Anna is twice referred to as "doomed," by Vronsky and later by his friend, Yashvin. She again seems to foresee her own demise in a scene in Italy, where the lovers are supposedly happy. She tells Vronsky they will be "punished" for being "too happy."[48]

The emphasis on punishment in this film is, of course, not entirely Breen's invention. It owes something to the original novel and, moreover, is perfectly consistent with the nineteenth-century convention of the fall. But the point is that under Breen's administration, this convention was taken as a paradigm for dealing with the problem of the ending. For, given the trajectory of the fall, the defense of a film was no longer contingent solely upon the final scene. Censorship became coextensive with the development of the plot as such.

One can begin to see why Breen decided to emphasize this particular case in his annual report to Hays. It indicates a decisive expansion of the range and scope of industry self-regulation. At the level of detail, the film barely hints at transgression. The heroine's consequent punishment is meticulously worked through the course of the narrative, in the organization of shots, individual scenes, and the more general trajectory of the action. Yet I want to suggest that even in a case like *Anna Karenina*, in which censorship was greatly refined and extended, it was possible to maneuver within and around its constraints. Unfortunately, the documentation relating to specific points of dispute and compromise between Breen and the producer is scanty. Breen, learning from Wingate's mistakes, perhaps, did not tend to discuss his difficulties with the studios in reports to Hays. But the film itself provides a source of evidence. It seems to me to move in directions that Breen's description does not acknowledge.

The limits of Breen's reading begin to emerge if we shift attention from the heroine's punishment to the more general problem of the couple. We have seen that self-regulation tended to place emphasis on the formation of the couple as a means of defense. If endings were important prior to 1934, it was partly because they entailed some sort of reconciliation between the sexes, so that sex roles were stabilized and a normative definition of the family could be advanced. In this particular case, however, there is a disjuncture between the formation of the couple and the enunciation of the values which censorship sought to reinforce. The driving force of the narrative lies in the attraction between Anna and Vronsky, not Anna and Karenin. The couple has itself become "deviant." It is for this reason, I think, that the film goes to such great lengths to condemn Anna and Vronsky, to assert what Breen calls the "sanctity of the marriage bond." However, the treatment of the love affair is much more ambiguous than Breen's description of the film would suggest. It is highly romanticized, and in this sense the "deviant" couple is simultaneously held up as an ideal.

During the scene at the opera, a woman remarks on Anna's beauty, saying that she and Vronsky are a "superb couple." While this remark is immediately denied—her companion retorts that they "aren't even a couple"—it carries a certain force in the context of the film as a whole. The idea of Anna and Vronsky as the perfect romantic couple is evoked in numerous ways, most obviously in dialogue. Scenes between Anna and Vronsky lapse into a rather florid prose style when the lovers declare their sentiments. For example, Vronsky declares to Anna that without her he is "doomed, doomed to unimaginable despair" or alternately, given her acquiescence, "bliss, bliss unimaginable." The invocation of fate here, as well as the use of repetition, is quite typical of the way in which the dialogue works to magnify the intensity and importance of the affair.

But visual style, not language, is the primary means of romanticizing the love affair. There are a number of scenes in which set design and costume set off Anna and Vronsky as a pair. Consider, for example, the garden party sequence. Greta Garbo and Fredric March are dressed entirely in white and lit much more brilliantly than the other actors within the scene (compare Figures 5.3 and 5.4). While playing croquet, they form a distinct tableau in contrast to the relatively dark figures which occupy the foreground of the shot (see Figures 5.1 and 5.2). Thus despite the fact that the scene is played from the point of view of the disapproving crowd, Garbo and March *look* like a "superb" couple.

The film also plays upon Garbo's image in ways which underscore and augment the love affair. For example, consider the highly charged moment of Vronsky's first meeting with Anna, at the train station. Having

5.3

5.4

seen his mother through one of the windows of the train, Vronsky approaches the doorway. But instead of his mother, Garbo/Anna appears, emerging out of a cloud of smoke (see Figure 5.5). The shot is of rather long duration, and is punctuated by a lush melody played on violin, the first music in a scene which has previously been limited to diegetic sound. This kind of dramatic introduction of the star is not untypical of Hollywood films of this period. What is important here is the insistence upon Vronsky's point of view. There are two cuts to a reverse angle which indicate she is the object of his gaze. Further, the unexpectedness of her appearance, the surprise, if you will, is an effect of Vronsky's position, his "expectations" within the story. Thus, the extreme idealization of Garbo's image—the smoke, the diffused lighting, the musical accompaniment—which is, in part, a function of her status as star, is also mediated by Vronsky's point of view. That is, the star's image is used to evoke the sudden fascination of the male character.

At various levels, then, dialogue, visual style, and the manipulation of Garbo's image give the relationship between Anna and Vronsky a

5.5

particularly intense emotional charge. But while the film exceeds the terms of Breen's description, this representation of the couple can ulti-mately be reconciled with the general impetus of censorship. That is, the highly romanticized treatment of the pair—what one might suppose the producers wanted—is finally made congruent with what Breen required: the heroine's denunciation and decline.

The romantic tradition does not, of course, require that love be happy or successful. In general, one finds an insistence upon the impossibility of achieving satisfaction, upon the inaccessibility or loss of the object of desire. *Anna Karenina* exploits this tradition to the point that one might even say that the film's romanticism is *predicated* on the heroine's suf-fering and decline. The punishment and condemnation of the heroine are coextensive with her idealization. This tendency is evident if we consider the visuals, and in particular the use of reaction shots. These close-ups, which call attention to the details of Garbo's highly nuanced perfor-mance, are pronounced at the moments of the character's loss: they highlight Anna's jealousy, the moments of her separation from Vronsky. For example, when Vronsky announces his intention to depart for the war, a series of relatively lengthy reaction shots emphasize the play of expression on Garbo's face (see Figures 5.6–5.8). Similarly, the final sequence at the train station, when Anna witnesses Vronsky bid farewell to his mother and the Princess Serokina, gives way to a close-up in which the actress mimes resignation and despair (see Figures 5.9a–5.9c). Thus, the moments in which Anna suffers, is "punished" in Breen's terms, are also those in which the close-ups dramatize the urgency and all-consuming nature of the heroine's passion.

The device of the fall thus provides a smooth reconciliation between what might otherwise have been conflicting pressures or tendencies within the film. Anna and Vronsky can be set up as the "perfect couple," while the impetus toward a normative definition of the family is satisfied through the emphasis upon the doomed and tragic nature of the affair. It is therefore impossible for us to isolate some kind of "offensive material" which remains external to, or undermines, the logic of the development of the plot. If the love affair is intensified and made attractive in ways Breen does not acknowledge in his report, its very intensity is, in part, a function of the scenario of the heroine's suffering and loss. The film

5.6

5.7

5.8

5.9a

5.9b

5.9c

does not work against the limitations of censorship so much as it seems to embrace them.

Thus, the reformulation of policy which took place under Breen, and in particular the treatment of narrative, served to extend and reinforce the emphasis upon the couple or the family which had been evident in only a fragmentary way in many of the fallen woman films of the early thirties. Rather than simply an ending which affirms the legitimacy of the couple, one finds the progressive unfolding of the plot working toward this end. This is not to suggest that after 1934 it became impossible for films to bypass the requirements of the Production Code Administration. Breen certainly did not get everything he wanted in negotiations with producers, especially once the worst of the crisis had passed. For example, in the case of the 1941 remake of *Back Street*, the studio declined to make the revisions requested by the Production Code Administration. Breen proposed that the illicit lovers undergo a fall—that the hero's death be motivated by his public "disgrace" while his mistress degenerated into a "cheap hag of a gambler."[49] The film does not take on this punitive cast, however. Indeed, in both the general contours of the plot and the treatment of detail, the 1941 remake follows closely upon the 1932 version. Nonetheless, it seems to me that after 1934 there was relatively less room within the fallen woman cycle to question, even indirectly, the values of work, chastity, or marriage. The requirements of the Production Code Administration were thoroughly integrated with conventions of narrative, and in this sense censorship became both more subtle and more pervasive.

6

Class and Glamour in the Films
of the Late Thirties

JOSEPH BREEN MAKES several notes which suggest that he was aware of the public criticisms directed toward the industry on the topic of luxury. A memo after a story conference on *Camille* states: "We should endeavor to tone down references to the effect that being a mistress is profitable."[1] In a review of *The Greeks Had a Word for Them*, written before he assumed control of the Production Code Administration, Breen complained: "The fact is *The Greeks Had a Word for Them* shows three young women, obviously prostitutes, living in luxury as a reward of their mode of living."[2] In the case of *Baby Face*, he noted more cryptically that it was "the kind or type of picture which ought not be encouraged."[3]

In contrast with the early thirties, there is a real alteration in the treatment of class rise in the films of the last half of the decade. Most obviously, censorship tempered the rapaciousness and aggressivity of the gold digger. For example, in *Mannequin* (MGM, 1937) the heroine rebels against the drudgery of her job and of working-class family life. She divorces a shiftless husband and marries a shipping tycoon. She does not seek this marriage, however; rather it is the tycoon who insists upon it. Further, she must continually fend off her ex-husband, who suspects her motives for remarriage and threatens to "expose" her as a gold digger. Thus, although the rise is accomplished in this instance, the central character does not actively pursue it. The film insists upon the heroine's genuine affection for her new husband and her lack of interest in money.

The treatment of the Mae West persona also changes in the later part of the decade, in keeping with the general transformation of the characterization of the gold digger. In *Belle of the Nineties* (1934), for instance, the West character decides to return the jewels that have been bestowed on her by an admirer. She explains to her maid that the sacrifice is necessary because she "would not make him happy." This decision is accompanied by the performance of a gospel number with a refrain that evokes the suicide motif reminiscent of earlier renditions of the genre: "I'm gonna drown down in those troubled waters that creep around my soul / Wash away my sins before the morning." In *Klondike Annie* (1936), the West character impersonates a settlement worker, Sister Annie, and is thereby reformed, even to the point of delivering a temperance lecture.

Censorship after 1934 did more than alter the characterization of the gold digger heroine, however. Under the pressure of Breen's notion of compensating moral values, representations of upward mobility became much more guarded and circumspect. In the most extreme cases, one finds an insistence upon the defeat of the heroine's social aspirations. Moreover, while the display of clothes and furnishings continued unabated within the Hollywood cinema as a whole, within the fallen woman cycle in particular, films began to call attention to, and critique, spectacles of consumption. I propose to trace this process in *Stella Dallas* and *Kitty Foyle*. Each of these films self-consciously refers to the treatment of class typical of the genre in the early thirties, and calls attention to the concept of glamour as such.

Stella Dallas

Feminist theorists and critics interested in the possibility of accounting for film spectatorship in terms of female fantasy have focused debate on the example of *Stella Dallas*.[4] My discussion of the film should be distinguished from this body of work in that it deals with the notion of spectatorship in a more restricted and historically localized sense. As I have noted, in the thirties, glamour was defined as a problem by reform groups and social scientists concerned about the Hollywood cinema's presumed appeal to women, particularly young, working-class women. Their conception of spectatorship was inscribed in some of the films of the period, most notably in the opening of *Stella Dallas*, in which Stella becomes enraptured by the image of upper-class life that she finds at the movies. I will argue that the film evoked this *idea* of the female spectator as part of a systematic strategy by which the representation of class rise was brought in line with the demands of censorship.

Stella Dallas does not appear to have contained material which industry censors regarded as potentially offensive. The script was approved by Breen without comment save for the emendation of one line of dialogue.[5] As in the case of *Anna Karenina*, then, one can pose the question of what made this script acceptable, even ideal, from the point of view of the Production Code Administration. In my view, the film undercut the motif of class rise in ways which made it highly congenial with the aims and interests of censorship.

The story opens with a rather meteoric rise. Stella, a poor girl from a factory town, manuevers herself into a marriage with the well-bred and faintly aristocratic Steven Dallas. Steven provides her with a large house, elaborate clothes, and an entrance into the town's most exclusive club. But, loud and vulgar, Stella finds it impossible to adjust to Steven's upper-class tastes and interests. They separate. Their daughter, Laurel, grows up with the social graces which enable her to fit into her father's world. However, Stella does not know how to dress or conduct herself in "polite" circles. She commits a series of faux pas which embarrass both Laurel and herself, and which gradually erode her social position. In one episode, the town gossips observe Stella on a train, seemingly intoxicated and laughing raucously in the company of the déclassé Ed Munn. As a result Stella is ostracized, and a party for the young Laurel is ruined when the guests—the students and teachers of Laurel's exclusive private school—fail to turn up.

In another episode, when Laurel is grown, Stella's behavior threatens to disrupt a budding romance between Laurel and the upper-class Richard Grosvenor III. At a fashionable summer resort, Stella is confined to her bed for the first portion of the holiday. In her absence Laurel is accepted by the upper-class families which frequent the hotel, and an engagement with Richard seems imminent. However, when Stella recovers and makes an appearance at the hotel, her dress and demeanor scandalize Laurel's new friends. In an attempt to prevent her mother from finding out she has been an object of ridicule and contempt, Laurel arranges their sudden departure from the hotel.

On the trip home, Stella overhears a conversation between two girls who intimate that the Grosvenors would never accept Laurel since she is saddled with such a "common creature" for a mother. In order to insure her daughter's success, Stella renounces all claim to her. She places Laurel under the care of her ex-husband's new, upper-class, wife. In the final scene of the film, Stella stands in the pouring rain, peering in the window of the elegant mansion in which her daughter is being married.

A self-conscious reference to the idea of luxury or glamour is made in an early scene, just prior to Stella's marriage. She attends the cinema with Steven. At the end of the film she sits transfixed, and then confesses she would like to emulate the "elegant and refined" characters she has just seen. Her marriage to the well-bred Dallas, then, in some sense takes place under the aegis of the cinema. The pursuit of Steven, and of money, is motivated by the attempt to embody a certain ideal of wealth and refinement which the cinema proffers.

In its treatment of this motif, the film inverts the pattern of the gold-digger films of the early thirties. In films like *The Easiest Way* or even *Blonde Venus,* class rise appears "effortless," a function of the seemingly instantaneous transformation of the heroine's dress and material surroundings. *Stella Dallas,* on the contrary, marks the failure of the heroine's social aspirations by rendering her transformation as a hideous display. This is most obvious in the scene at the resort in which, after a series of scenes showing Stella shopping and being made up, she makes an appearance at the hotel. She wears extremely high heels covered with sea shells, a floral print dress with ruffles and black lace, a black hat in the shape of a giant bow, and a white fur wrap with the animal's head and feet intact (see Figure 6.1). She speaks too loudly, calls the waiter "Boy," and tips lavishly, inappropriately. The scene is an almost perfect reversal of the kind of transformation that we find in a film like *The Easiest Way,* in which the heroine appears in the height of fashion, at one with her new surroundings. The failure of the transformation goes beyond the sense that Stella looks out of place or lacks a knowledge of hotel etiquette. Her image is debased, charged with what, in the terms of the film, are negative sexual connotations. While these implications are never directly stated as such in the dialogue, I think the preponderance of black net in Stella's costume, the sheer ostentatiousness of the display, and the exaggerated movement of the actress's hips and arms when she walks, recall the look of a streetwalker. The ambiguity of Stella's position is evident, too, in the adjective "common" which one of the upper-class women applies to her. For "common" can be understood in the sense of working-class, but also in the sense of sexually promiscuous.

Of course, one of the ironies of the film is that, from the point of view of the spectator, Stella is virtually asexual, only concerned with her

6.1 *Stella Dallas*. Publicity still

daughter. That is, the spectator is able to interpret her actions in ways
that the upper-class characters within the diegesis can not. So, for
example, in the scene with Ed Munn on the train, at the very moment in
which she is being suspected of adultery by several of the upper-class
passengers, she tells Ed, "There isn't a man alive who could get me
going anymore." But even though, for the spectator, Stella is exculpated
and even idealized as a mother, the film consistently demonstrates that

her upper-class pretensions are untenable. And this process is most obvious in the debasement of her *image*: she embodies a travesty of glamour, her appearance coded simultaneously as lower-class ("overdone") and sexually transgressive ("cheap").

I would hypothesize that the debasement of the heroine, and the concomitant insistence upon the barriers to class rise, made the film acceptable, indeed an ideal case, from the point of view of industry censorship. Not only does the film undercut Stella's social aspirations, but it establishes a clear demarcation between the "natural" decorum and restraint of upper-class women (such as Laurel and her stepmother) and the irredeemable vulgarity of Stella's display of her own body. The appearance if not the "fact" of some impropriety marks Stella's failure in society; it is the principal way in which her pretensions are parodied.

It might be argued that in contradistinction to the general trajectory of the narrative, the ending of the film provides a mediated form of class rise. For example, critic Linda Williams has argued that Stella's ambitions are finally realized via a process of substitution in which Laurel attains the position her mother could not.[6] The film ends, as it began, with the motif of Stella as spectator. The exclusive wedding, situated in the imposing interior of Laurel's stepmother's mansion, and set off in the window frame *as* an image, echoes the vision of upper-class life which initially fascinated Stella at the movies. Paradoxically, while Stella is excluded from the final scene, her desire is nonetheless represented there. In this sense, the ending of *Stella Dallas* can be interpreted as a triumph for the heroine.

I would agree with Williams that the film establishes a relationship of substitution between mother and daughter, and to this extent Stella's aspirations are realized in the final scene. However, given the genre conventions, and the conception of female spectatorship, to which the film itself alludes, I would argue that the motif of class rise has been transformed, "sanitized" as it were, in crucial ways. The film evokes the whole tradition of maternal sacrifice in order finally to purge Stella's ambition of any suggestion of impropriety or exploitation. Stella engineers the wedding by renouncing all connection to her daughter and her former husband (her source of income). As in the familiar *Madame X* story, she is left alone, reduced to poverty and virtual anonymity. The spectacle appears as the result, indeed the confirmation, of this sacrifice. Because Stella's ambition is realized indirectly, through Laurel, it can be made perfectly congruent with her domestic role. Brought within the purview of the family, the rise is thus stripped of its threatening aspect, of the connotations of female aggressivity and sexual deviance.

Kitty Foyle

In contrast with *Stella Dallas*, *Kitty Foyle* is a case which posed difficulties for the Production Code Administration. It concerns a love affair between a "white collar girl" and the scion of a wealthy Philadelphia family. While Breen was ostensibly concerned only with the representation of illicit sexuality in this case, the inclusion of "compensating moral values" inevitably had consequences for the representation of class. Thus it is possible to document with some precision how the Production Code Administration's policies and procedures impinged upon the trajectory of the rise.

The film derives from a novel by Christopher Morley published in 1939. Written in the first person, the novel comprises a series of loosely connected episodes, the heroine's memories. Like the novel, the film evokes the process of reminiscence. It opens with a frame story in which Kitty must choose between marriage to Mark, a struggling young doctor, and going to South America with Wyn, the wealthy man with whom she has been in love for most of her life. Recollections of her relationship with each of these men are presented in a series of flashbacks. The flashbacks follow one another in a linear sequence so that the effect of the whole is a single, continuous narrative, punctuated by voice-over commentary from the perspective of the present. The end of one flashback is distinguished from the beginning of another by the repeated image of a glass paperweight showing a little girl on a sleigh in a snowstorm.

Kitty Foyle, of Irish immigrant stock, grows up in Philadelphia. As a child she is fascinated by the "Mainliners," the wealthy and well-established families of the town. As a young woman, Kitty obtains work as a stenographer on a magazine that is run by Wyn Stafford, one of Philadelphia's elite. The two become lovers and she tells her father that she expects a proposal. However, Wyn's magazine folds and it becomes clear that he does not intend to propose marriage. Following the death of her father, Kitty departs for New York in search of a job.

In New York, Kitty joins what the voice-over calls the "white collar brigade." She works for a cosmetics firm and lives in straitened circumstances, sharing an apartment with two other working women. She begins to date Mark, who, to her dismay, does not even buy her dinner on their first night together (in a backhanded compliment, one of her roommates observes that the only good thing that can be said about the doctor is that he saves his money). Wyn seeks her out, and in a decided contrast with the doctor, entertains her lavishly. He finally proposes and they are married.

The couple returns to Philadelphia where Wyn's family proposes to "remake" Kitty—send her to finishing school and to Europe—in order to make her acceptable to their set. Kitty refuses, and realizing that Wyn is not able to defy his family's wishes, opts for a divorce. Kitty returns to New York where she discovers that she is pregnant. She has hopes of remarriage until she discovers through the newspaper that Wyn has become engaged to a woman of his own class. She conceals the fact of her pregnancy from Wyn. Her baby is born dead. Sent back to Philadelphia by the cosmetics firm, Kitty is called upon to serve Wyn's new wife and realizes that they have a child. This concludes the final flashback and the film returns to the present, where the frame story is resolved by Kitty's decision to marry Mark.

Breen's initial correspondence with the producer concerned a synopsis of the Morley novel.[7] Breen warned that the novel was unacceptable under the Code because Wyn and Kitty had "frequent illicit sex affairs" (in the novel they do not marry) and Kitty aborted her illegitimate child.[8] He cautioned that the story would have to be rewritten so that these elements could be eliminated. Following negotiations, the abortion was taken out of the story and Wyn and Kitty were married, thereby making the baby "legitimate."[9] Despite Breen's objections, however, the producers refrained from altering a scene between Wyn and Kitty, before the marriage, in which they spend the evening alone in a cabin in the Poconos. While the scene does not make their affair explicit, the implication seems unmistakable. The pair sit in front of a fire and the scene ends with a kiss and a slow fade-out which Breen found suggestive of a "sex affair."[10] Certainly, the representation of illicit sexuality at this relatively late date (1940) is much less ambiguous than in films produced at the peak of the public crisis such as *Anna Karenina* (1935) or *Camille* (1937).

In its treatment of detail, then, the film was at the limits of what was considered acceptable by the Production Code Administration. Breen therefore sought to amend the narrative as a whole to compensate for the inclusion of this material. He informed the producers that they would have to observe what he called a "formula" for the representation of illicit love affairs:

> The illicit sex affair must be shown affirmatively to be "wrong." It must not be "condoned nor justified, nor made to appear right and acceptable," and the sinners must be "punished."[11]

Several of the events of the story can be construed, in accordance with Breen's requirements, as punishment of the heroine. The death of Kitty's child, for example, does not simply alleviate the need to show abortion within the film; it also constitutes one of the unhappy consequences of the affair. Kitty's treatment by Wyn's family and the loss of Wyn to another woman can also be seen as a form of punishment, in Breen's terms. The film does not highlight the heroine's suffering or self-abnegation to the same degree as does *Stella Dallas* or *Anna Karenina*, however, and an examination of the progressive revisions of the script suggests that other devices were employed to render the love affair acceptable to the Production Code Administration.

A comparison of the novel, the first version of the script by Donald Ogden Stewart, and the second version by Dalton Trumbo[12] shows that the major revisions are not at the level of plot—all of the drafts of the screenplay follow the events of the novel quite closely—but rather have to do with the mode of narration of these events.[13] The novel proceeds more or less linearly beginning with Kitty's memories of childhood. In contrast, the screenplay is composed of a series of flashbacks which, in both drafts, is initiated by the frame story that poses the question of whether Kitty should run away with Wyn or marry Mark. (In addition, Dalton Trumbo adds still another framing device, a putative historical prologue on the "white collar girl".) The frame story serves as a vehicle for introducing commentary and criticism of the heroine's actions, and in this regard meets Breen's requirements that the love affair "be shown affirmatively to be wrong."

In the frame story, Kitty stands before her bedroom mirror, preparing to run off with Wyn. Her reflected image comes to life and begins to argue with her, advocating marriage to Mark and cautioning against the continuation of the affair: "Maybe 'wife' isn't the most romantic title in the world. But it's comfortable, honey, and it's respectable and it IS a title." The story as a whole is motivated by Kitty's "debate" with her mirror image which thus becomes central to the film's system of address. The mirror image addresses the "real" Kitty in the commentary which initiates each flashback, and it sets up the narrative as an act of moral self-examination: "Well you'd better take a little time, sister, because forever is a long, long time and it never hurts to check with the conductor to see if you are on the right train." Kitty must remember her past in order to reach a decision concerning the "proper" course of conduct in the present. Thus, not only is there a stated endorsement of matrimony, but *the narration of the story as such,* "remembering the past" in the terms of the fiction, leads Kitty to opt for marriage. The story which is told—of the illicit love affair—is in this sense undermined by the circumstances of the narration.

The system of address established through the frame story thus fulfills a strategic function, offsetting or compensating for the potentially offensive aspects of the love affair. While this device does not directly bear on the problem of money or luxury within the film, the second major revision made by the screenwriters is primarily concerned with the representation of class. The second draft of the script, by Dalton Trumbo, alters the role of Kitty's father, "Pop," in order to introduce an extended criticism of Kitty's relationship with Wyn. A comparison with the first draft, by Donald Ogden Stewart, indicates the direction of the change. In the Stewart version, as well as the original novel, Pop encourages unconventional behavior. When a school official calls to complain about the young Kitty's conduct, Pop chases him out of the house, shouting, "I don't care what rule it is, we Foyles don't conform if we don't want to." At no point does he discuss Kitty's relationship with Wyn. In contrast, in Trumbo's version of the script, Pop operates as the vehicle of what Breen might have considered a "voice of morality." He does not denounce the affair in moral terms, however, but rather comments at length on the difficulties of marrying out of one's own class. For example, he counsels Kitty that men of Wyn's set "always wind up marrying one of their own kind." In an earlier sequence, he admonishes the young Kitty for showing interest in the activities of the Philadelphia Mainliners. In the same scene, he denounces the writers of what he calls "Cinderella stories":

> Writing those clap trap stories about Cinderella and princes, and poisoning the minds of innocent children! Putting crazy ideas in girl's heads! Making them dissatisfied with honest shoe clerks and bookkeepers! Why they're the ruination of more girls than forty actors.

He goes on to present his own version of the end of the fairy tale, in which, after marriage to the prince, Cinderella discovers that they have nothing in common to talk about. The two end up in divorce court, "with Cinderella saying he hit her on the head with the glass slipper, and the prince saying the whole thing was a dirty frame-up!"

Pop's counter-fairy tale is, of course, borne out by the trajectory of the narrative: class differences separate Kitty and her "prince" and the two end up in divorce court. The authority of Pop's warning is heightened since at several points he is doubled with Kitty's mirror image, the incarnation of the agency of the narration. The film allies Pop and Kitty's alter ego through the repeated use of the glass paperweight, a gift to Kitty from her father, which accompanies the voice-over that punctuates the transition between flashbacks. Moreover, the first flashback underscores the association between Pop and Kitty's mirror image through the repetition of dialogue. During the course of the initial debate on marriage, Kitty challenges her alter ego: "Well, I think you're wrong." The mirror image reminds her that she has said this phrase once before, to her father, and this initiates the flashback in which Kitty objects to her father's discussion of *Cinderella*. Thus, Pop's diatribe, which mitigates the appeal of the upper-class man, buttresses the defense of marriage proposed within the frame story.

While Breen did not discuss the problem of money or luxury in his correspondence with producers, I think we can surmise that the difficulty posed by the representation of illicit sexuality in this case was, in large part, the allure of the rise. For the logic of the revisions introduced by the screenwriters constituted a defense against the allure of becoming rich through men, the "Cinderella story." One of the most interesting aspects of the case is the persistence with which the film adheres to this motif, in spite of the highly guarded or defensive mode in which it is played out. The film goes to great lengths to establish that Kitty is not interested in men for financial gain, that is, to distinguish her from the stereotypical gold digger. Thus, Mark explains his unwillingness to spend money on Kitty on their first date as a "test" which confirms that she is not a gold digger. In a later confrontation with Wyn's family, Kitty herself asserts that she did not marry him for his money. Despite these gestures of denial, however, there are a number of ways in which the film plays on the appeal of the idea of marrying a rich man.[14]

One sequence in particular, the flashback in which Wyn seeks out Kitty in New York, seems to defy the general impetus of censorship. The sequence clearly echoes the outline of the fairy tale *Cinderella*. Wyn, simultaneously in the role of prince and fairy godmother, appears unexpectedly, provides Kitty with a new dress, and takes her to a ball. The dialogue tends to reinforce this parallel. One of her roommates suggests that Kitty is waiting for Wyn to "rescue" her from her mundane routine. He is even referred to as her "knight in shining armor."

The references to *Cinderella* are not the only way in which the film evokes the appeal of moving up in class. Beyond this, the opposition between Mark's penuriousness and Wyn's liberality unmistakably points to the attractiveness of the latter. This becomes clear if we consider the visual design of the segment. Kitty and Mark are shown in drab and rather shabby surroundings: a dark and crowded subway, Kitty's small and crowded apartment (see Figure 6.2). In contrast, her date with Wyn is characterized by the kind of lavish display typical of the gold-digger films of the early thirties. In one of the instantaneous transformations typical of the genre, Wyn alters the look of Kitty's apartment, filling it with flowers (see Figures 6.3 and 6.4). The display of clothing and decor in this instance is accompanied by what the reviewer for the *American Cinematographer* described as the "spectacular lighting" of the scenes in

6.2 *Kitty Foyle*

6.3 *Kitty Foyle*

6.4 *Kitty Foyle*

wealthy surroundings.[15] The low-key lighting of the interior of Kitty's apartment (indeed of most of the interiors in the film) gives way to the scene at the ball which is brightly illuminated. The scene has a distinctive glow, the aura of glamour (see Figure 6.5).

At the level of visual style, then, *Kitty Foyle* clearly plays upon the appeal of the rise. The question is to what extent this destabilizes the normative view of both marriage and work which the film affirms through the frame story and the character of Pop. I would argue that in this instance the narrative works to offset or contain the potentially subversive implications of glamour or display. Indeed, this example indicates the extent to which censorship came to rely upon, and was integrated within, the mechanisms of narrative.

The segment in which Wyn takes Kitty to the ball is undercut by the retrospective logic of the narration. In the frame story it is obvious that the affair has gone awry: Kitty lives in an extremely modest boarding house and Wyn is married to someone else. The film brackets off the episode of Kitty's transformation as a failed aspiration, a memory quite removed from her circumstances in the present. Moreover, Kitty's aspirations are critiqued by various references to the Cinderella story. The film enacts a glamorous rise while at the same time, as a defensive

6.5 *Kitty Foyle*

maneuver, setting it off *as fantasy,* an attempt to live out a little girl's fairy tale. The contours of this strategy become apparent if we consider the voice-over's commentary on the sequence in which Wyn comes to New York and takes Kitty out dancing. On the dance floor in the early hours of the morning, Kitty tells Wyn that "in five minutes the alarm will be going off." When he proposes marriage, she repeats the metaphor: "Dear God, don't ring the alarm clock now, for just a little while." The next flashback, which concerns the breakup of Kitty's marriage, begins with the voice-over's comment: "But the alarm did ring. It had a funny little jangle and you seemed to hear it all the way to Philadelphia." Thus, the evening with Wyn is explicitly identified with a dream state. Given the use of the voice-over, the events which follow—Kitty's treatment by Wyn's family and her divorce—are posited as the reassertion of the everyday, "waking up." Not only is the heroine punished, in Breen's terms, through the divorce, the death of the child, and Wyn's remarriage, but also the voice-over narration gives this succession of events the inevitability of the real. The fairy-tale motif permits a very neat compromise between the aims of producers, who one can imagine sought to include the conventional use of spectacle or display, and the aims of censors, who sought to downplay the appeal of the illicit love affair. Although the idea of the rise is made attractive in this case, the development of the plot, which follows the trajectory of Kitty's growth from child to woman, tends toward the choice of Mark, the formation of the "legitimate" couple, as the final achievement of maturity.

While *Kitty Foyle* clearly posed greater difficulties for the Production Code Administration than *Stella Dallas,* the films treat class in similar ways, deflecting the trajectory of the heroine's ascent. *Stella Dallas begins* with the heroine's acquisition of money, and the development of the plot is concerned with the gradual *erosion* of her social position. In *Kitty Foyle,* the use of the voice-over and the retrospective organization of the narrative also militate against the rise. There are many other examples of films from the later thirties which thwart the heroine's aspirations. *Alice Adams,* which was not only approved but actually commended by Breen, concerns a girl of modest circumstances who aspires to attract a wealthy beau. As in *Stella Dallas,* the film is primarily concerned with her inability to live up to an image of wealth and refinement. In one sequence, in which the beau has been invited to dinner, the maid hired for the day proves incompetent, and family members prove irredeemably gross, e.g., her father's starched shirtfront bursts open at the table.

In several of the films made in the late thirties and early forties, the conventions of the cycle are reworked within a new generic context—the atmosphere of pessimism and angst characteristic of film noir. In *Marked Woman*, Mary works as a hostess in a nightclub which is taken over by the notorious gangster Johnny Vanning. She announces her intention to play along with the crook and use him for her own ends:

> We've all tried this twelve-and-a-half-a-week stuff. It's no good. Living in furnished rooms. Walking to work. Going hungry a couple of days a week so you can have some clothes to put on your back. I've had enough of that for the rest of my life. . . . I know all the angles. And I think I'm smart enough to keep one step ahead of them until I get enough to pack it all in and live on easy street the rest of my life. I know how to beat this racket.

Mary's collaboration with Vanning leads to the murder of her younger sister, and her own beating and disfigurement at his hands. She is led to admit that she did not "know all the angles," and accepts the death of her sister as her own punishment. The ending of the film, in which she regretfully walks away from the young district attorney who has championed her interests in court, emphasizes the differences of class and status which serve as barriers to a "legitimate" marriage, and hence, to social mobility.

Another instance of the influence of film noir, *The Hard Way*, clearly reformulated the title and basic trajectory of *The Easiest Way*. The story is narrated in flashback by an older woman who has just attempted suicide. She had set out to make her young sister-in-law a success on the stage. In the classic pattern, the two had escaped from a small factory town and, using various men, made their way to New York where they scored a hit in a musical comedy. Their success was undermined by a series of dire events. The older woman's ruthlessness and ambition stood in the way of the young actress's marriage and threatened her mental stability. After a spectacular failure in a dramatic role, the younger woman abandoned her career in favor of marriage, forsaking the partnership and leading the older woman to seek her own death.

The textual analyses proposed here give some account of how the treatment of class altered across the course of the nineteen thirties, that is, they suggest why censorship became more "powerful," in a rhetorical sense, after 1934. One of the greatest contrasts between the films of the early thirties and those of the later period lies in the form of what industry censors called the "voice of morality." Prior to 1934, this device was a relatively isolated component of the narrative—a single character would chastize the heroine in one or possibly two scenes. After 1934, the function of criticizing the heroine was no longer limited to the speech of a character but was figured at a more abstract and impersonal level through the mechanisms of narration. In *Anna Karenina,* for example, the voice of morality is elaborated through the manipulation of character point of view. The initiation of the love affair is viewed largely from the point of view of Karenin and other members of his social set, a mode of narration which stresses their growing suspicion and disapproval. In *Kitty Foyle,* the warnings and cautions of Kitty's mirror image serve as a pretext for the narration of the story as such. Through the system of flashbacks and the use of voice-over, the narrative is presented in the form of a moral lesson which ultimately leads the heroine to renounce her former lover and repudiate her own story. In both of these cases, then, the values affirmed by individual characters are also reinforced at a structural level, through the way in which the story is told.

This technique for rendering judgments upon the heroine differs significantly from the didactic speeches typical of the early period. The spectator might well disagree with an explicit endorsement of marriage or, as Breen points out in a discussion of the role of Karenin in *Anna Karenina,* find the character who delivers such a speech unsympathetic, but insofar as the judgments are *implicit* within a film's system of address, they become much more difficult to deny. In the case of *Kitty Foyle,* one may well dislike Pop as a character, but given a certain position of knowledge, articulated through the device of the voice-over, one might nonetheless assume his point of view and the moral position vis-à-vis the heroine that this implies. Censorship becomes more pervasive then, as the process of rendering judgment is "hidden" within the mechanisms of narration.

This description of the rhetoric of censorship is crucial to our understanding of its ideological effects. After 1934, the films within the cycle are relatively more unified; they appear to proceed inevitably and "naturally" toward the final moment of closure. Theorists such as Stephen Heath and Raymond Bellour have analyzed, in great detail, the *systematicity* of the classical Hollywood cinema, that is, the principles of redundancy, of movement across multiple levels of signification, which produce the effect of linearity and unity.[16] My claim is that these textual processes fulfilled a defensive function at a particular moment in history. They served as a mechanism for absorbing and negotiating material which, in the period, was constituted as "difficult" or "dangerous." Thus, for example, in the face of the potentially destabilizing effects of the rise, *Kitty Foyle* motivates the formation of the legitimate couple in multiple ways, through various narrative devices. Of course, marriage is directly endorsed by Kitty's alter ego in the argument which forms the premise of the narration. It is also motivated, in more indirect fashion, by the fairy-tale motif which situates the illicit love affair in the realm of childhood and fantasy. What I want to emphasize here is the tremendous economy through which the film produces the sense of the inevitability of the final moment of closure. Even a seemingly arbitrary detail can contribute to this effect. For example, the repeated use of the glass paperweight in *Kitty Foyle*, which shows a little girl on a sleigh ride, functions to set up the ending in terms of Kitty "growing up."

I do not mean to propose that the strategies of censorship became perfectly coherent after 1934. A defensive process, self-regulation presupposed a compromise between conflicting forces or tendencies and thus was always potentially disunified. In the films of the late thirties, however, the compromises between the aims of producers and the MPPDA took the form of a reorganization of the overall trajectory of the plot. The devices which compensated for the heroine's transgressions were reiterated across the course of the story and developed through a variety of formal means—the debased and humiliating spectacle of the woman in *Stella Dallas*, the use of flashbacks and voice-over narration in *Kitty Foyle*. Even what were considered disruptive or offensive elements were integrated, at some level, within the logic of the narrative development. So, for example, the transformation scene in *Kitty Foyle* is marked as fantasy, leading toward the moment in which Kitty "wakes up" to the necessity of choosing Mark over Wyn. As self-regulation became more entrenched after 1934, it reinforced patterns of narrative development, of formal unity and closure, typical of the classical Hollywood cinema as a whole. These formal systems unobtrusively circumscribed the representation of female aggressivity, ambition, and illicit sexuality.

7

Afterword

Speaking to the directors, I appealed to their ingenuity and
artistic pride, hinting that it takes vastly more artistry to be
interesting while observing decent limits than when being risqué.
I told them, for example, that instead of seeing how far they
could get an actress to lift her skirt and still stay within the law
they might try seeing how low she could leave her skirts and still
maintain audience interest.

WILL HAYS

THE MODEL OF self-regulation as a process of negotiation suggests an
alternative to traditional ways of conceptualizing the history of film censorship. Considered as examples of "pre-Code" cinema, the films of the
late twenties and early thirties are usually characterized as raw, subversive, precisely *uncensored*.[1] In pointing to the fact that industry self-
regulation was at least operative by 1930, I have sought to modify the
grounds of this periodization, and the critical perspective it implies.

I have argued that self-regulation was always complicit to some
degree with the aims of the major film producers. That is, the MPPDA
sought to allow producers maximal use of their original material while at
the same time seeking to minimize the grounds for outside interference
in the distribution and exhibition of features. But if industry censors
never simply blocked the representation of offensive material, then by
the same logic, film producers did not give rise to what might be considered "free speech" in the legal sense of the term. Screenwriters and
directors devised stories in cognizance of the MPPDA's policies and procedures. They may have negotiated more or less amicably, and with
more or less success, but they could not ignore the MPPDA's rules for
shaping narrative and activating genre conventions. The fallen woman
films of the early thirties are thus not beyond censorship, but rather they
engage different forms of it than their counterparts from the latter part of
the decade.

The films made prior to 1934 seem quite explicit when compared
with those of the late thirties because of the Studio Relations Committee's policies and procedures on the treatment of detail. Industry censors
and producers arrived at compromises for indicating scenes of adultery,
seduction, and sexual exchange which often *permitted* filmmakers to
heighten the sense of the heroine's transgressiveness. For example, not
only does *Baby Face* utilize indirect means to suggest illicit sexuality,
but it often exploits the prohibitions of the Code for comic effect. Thus,
James Wingate's insistence that Warners refrain from showing Lily seducing men at the bank simply reinforced a running gag—the use of the
song "St. Louis Woman" and the tilt up the bank building to signal Lily's
adventures. In this instance, the very bar on direct representation precipitated a sly and sexually knowing joke. While it did not rely upon
innuendo, *Blonde Venus* also capitalized upon the Studio Relations Committee's preference for indirect modes of representation. For example,
the decision to excise the scenes which explained Helen's reasons for
sleeping with Nick helped to motivate the initiation of the love affair in
terms of the performance of the "Hot Voodoo" number, and the excessive
desire of the Blonde Venus. Although individual industry censors may
well have disapproved of *Blonde Venus* or *Baby Face*, the films employed
rhetorical subterfuges which were the logical extension of self-regulatory
practices. The explicitness of the early thirties cinema arises from the
textual dynamic of censorship.

The Studio Relations Committee's procedures for dealing with the
fallen woman plot, like its treatment of detail, permitted filmmakers
simultaneously to observe and circumvent the Code's limits. Its procedures for dealing with narrative in this period are best understood in the
context of the particular problems posed by genre conventions. Given
concerns about the effects of movies on young women, reformers and
industry censors focused attention on the fallen woman's luxurious life-
style. In the late thirties, their influence made itself felt in the quietist
and moralizing voice-over narration of *Kitty Foyle*, or the cruel under-
cutting of the heroine's aspirations in films like *Stella Dallas* and *Alice
Adams*. The films of the early thirties differ markedly from the later ones
in their vivid and unabashed evocations of social mobility. Transformation scenes stressing elegant clothes and modernist decor dramatized
alterations in the heroine's status. Moreover, many films, including both
The Easiest Way and *Baby Face*, set up the heroine's ambitiousness with
openings which depicted working-class life as miserable, squalid, and

degrading. This emphasis on class rise helped to construct the immoral, cynical, and sexually aggressive gold digger as a heroic figure. Given the industry's Production Code, which stated that sin should not be made attractive, and crime could not pay, how was this possible?

Because the Studio Relations Committee focused primarily on denunciation scenes and endings, it could tolerate forms of the plot which would have been unacceptable after 1934. For example, the last scene of *Baby Face*, which describes Lily's fall and domestication, remains markedly at odds with the way the film systematically develops the theme of her upward mobility. In general, the strategies of censorship in this period are not very well integrated within film narrative, are often transparently recognizable as such. The films shift abruptly between the story of the rise and scenes which could be construed as meeting the requirements of the Code. Dire warnings to the heroine are inserted without prior motivation, and endings often appear stressed or arbitrary.

The hollow, perfunctory quality of the ending of many early thirties fallen woman films follows directly not from the studio's original script but rather from the pattern of narrative development put in place by self-regulation itself. While the MPPDA typically advocated the heroine's punishment, the studios preferred the heroine to renounce her riches in favor of true love, as in the case of the studio's first draft of *Baby Face*. Even the "uncensored," happy endings endorsed by the studios entailed a reinstatement of moral and sexual norms through the formation of the couple. In the cases of both *Baby Face* and *Blonde Venus*, however, this reinforcement of sexual norms was vitiated by the films' adherence to the Studio Relations Committee's requirements. The insertion of seemingly unmotivated denunciation scenes in *Baby Face*, and the discrepancy between the logic of the narrative progression and the ending, call attention to the artificiality of these devices. Indeed, the punitive tone of the ending heightens the sense of the discrepancy between the final scenes and the story of the heroine's rise. Similarly, in *Blonde Venus*, the heroine's reformation, and even the attendant formation of the couple, do not follow logically, "naturally" from the rest of the story.

Thus, even the most contested and aberrant examples of the fallen woman film from the early thirties can be seen as constructs of censorship. If such films were able to question the sexual status quo, it was because the Studio Relations Committee's practices brought to the fore, and in some cases even intensified, the very conflicts around the genre which it had sought to contain. One of the most important effects of self-regulation after 1934 was to flatten out these sorts of conflicts. The power of the Production Code Administration after 1934 lay in its capacity to integrate its requirements within the body of the narrative, smoothing over the disjuncture between the story of the rise and the moral imperatives of the Code. The forms of censorship adopted under the Production Code Administration produced more unified and harmonious texts, abjuring the double meanings, the calculated ambiguities, and the narrative disjunctures which gave the films of the early thirties their zest.

To study the process of self-regulation, then, is to restore some sense of the difficulties which the representation of sexuality posed within the institutional matrix defined by the relations between external agencies, film producers, and industry censors. In the face of the continual process of dispute and negotiation which the fallen woman cycle brought into play, we can begin to envision femininity as a construct that was at once tenuous and overdetermined in highly complicated ways. We must take account of this process, I would maintain, if we are to fairly gauge the possibilities of resistance within the confines of the studio system, and within the parameters of the classical text. By looking at the arena in which battles were lost, and sometimes won, we can begin to imagine how things might have happened otherwise.

APPENDIX
NOTES
BIBLIOGRAPHY
INDEX

APPENDIX
CENSORSHIP CASES REVIEWED

This does not comprise a comprehensive filmography of fallen woman films, but rather a list of the cases reconstructed on the basis of the MPPDA censorship files and studio production records. Other films cited are given in the Index.

Two principal sources informed the composition of this sample. The first source was critical writing on the genre, most importantly, the wide range of films cited by Christian Viviani and Betsy McLane. The second source was MPPDA correspondence: the weekly reports to Hays which described "sex pictures" under review by the Studio Relations Committee, lists prepared by Breen in 1934–35 of films he wanted withdrawn from theaters, and the titles discussed in Breen's annual reports to Hays. The sample was further augmented by films which stirred public controversy in the period. For example, the relatively low ratings given to *Kitty Foyle* and *Two-Faced Woman* by the Catholic Legion of Decency led me to examine those cases.

As I have already noted, the MPPDA's definition of the "sex picture" encompassed gold-digger films which we would consider comedies. At the risk of blurring genre distinctions, I have retained this classificatory schema, because the comedic variants of the fallen woman plot consistently posed problems for Jason Joy. Similarly, I have included several screwball comedies within the sample to indicate the Production Code Administration's difficulties with such comedic variants. One of these, *The Miracle of Morgan's Creek* (1944), falls outside the strict bounds of my periodization, but is given here for its particularly deft handling of genre conventions in relation to censorship.

Alice Adams. 1935. RKO. George Stevens, dir. With Katharine Hepburn and Fred MacMurray.
An American Tragedy. 1931. Paramount. Joseph von Sternberg, dir. With Sylvia Sidney and Phillips Holmes.

Anna Karenina. 1935. MGM. Clarence Brown, dir. With Greta Garbo and Fredric March.

Ann Vickers. 1933. RKO. John Cromwell, dir. With Irene Dunne and Walter Huston.

The Awful Truth. 1937. Columbia. Leo McCarey, dir. With Irene Dunne, Cary Grant, and Ralph Bellamy.

Baby Face. 1933. Warner Brothers. Alfred Green, dir. With Barbara Stanwyck and George Brent.

Bachelor Mother. 1939. RKO. Garson Kanin, dir. With Ginger Rogers and David Niven.

Back Street. 1932. Universal. John Stahl, dir. With Irene Dunne and John Boles.

Back Street. 1941. Universal. Robert Stevenson, dir. With Margaret Sullavan and Charles Boyer.

Bed of Roses. 1933. RKO. Gregory La Cava, dir. With Constance Bennett and Joel McCrea.

Belle of the Nineties. 1934. Paramount. Leo McCarey, dir. With Mae West.

Blonde Venus. 1932. Paramount. Joseph von Sternberg, dir. With Marlene Dietrich, Herbert Marshall, and Cary Grant.

Blondie Johnson. 1933. Warner Brothers. Ray Enright, dir. With Joan Blondell and Chester Morris.

Born to Be Bad. 1934. 20th Century/United Artists. Lowell Sherman, dir. With Loretta Young and Cary Grant.

Born to Love. 1931. RKO. Paul Stein, dir. With Constance Bennett and Joel McCrea.

Call Her Savage. 1932. Fox. John Francis Dillion, dir. With Clara Bow.

Camille. 1937. MGM. George Cukor, dir. With Greta Garbo and Robert Taylor.

Christopher Strong. 1933. RKO. Dorothy Arzner, dir. With Katharine Hepburn and Colin Clive.

City Streets. 1931. Paramount. Rouben Mamoulian, dir. With Sylvia Sidney and Gary Cooper.

Comet over Broadway. 1938. Warner Brothers. Busby Berkeley, dir. With Kay Francis and Ian Hunter.

Common Clay. 1930. Fox. Victor Fleming, dir. With Constance Bennett.

Confession. 1937. Warner Brothers. Joe May, dir. With Kay Francis and Basil Rathbone.

Disgraced. 1933. Paramount. Erle Kenton, dir. With Helen Twelvetrees.

Dishonored. 1931. Paramount. Joseph von Sternberg, dir. With Marlene Dietrich and Victor McLaglen.

Dr. Monica. 1934. Warner Brothers. William Keighley, dir. With Kay Francis and Warren Williams.

The Easiest Way. 1931. MGM. Jack Conway, dir. With Constance Bennett, Robert Montgomery, and Adolphe Menjou.

East Is West. 1930. Universal. Monta Bell, dir. With Lupe Velez, Lew Ayres, and Edward G. Robinson.

Ex-Lady. 1933. Warner Brothers. Robert Florey, dir. With Bette Davis and Gene Raymond.

Female. 1933. Warner Brothers. Michael Curtiz and William Dieterle, dirs. With Ruth Chatterton and George Brent.

Fifth Avenue Girl. 1939. RKO. Gregory La Cava, dir. With Ginger Rogers and Walter Connolly.

Frisco Jenny. 1933. Warner Brothers. William Wellman, dir. With Ruth Chatterton.

Gallant Lady. 1933. 20th Century/United Artists. Gregory La Cava, dir. With Ann Harding.

Girls on Probation. 1938. Warner Brothers. William McGann, dir. With Jane Bryan and Ronald Reagan.

The Great Lie. 1941. Warner Brothers. Edmund Goulding, dir. With Bette Davis and Mary Astor.

The Greeks Had a Word for Them. 1932. Samuel Goldwyn/United Artists. Lowell Sherman, dir. With Madge Evans, Joan Blondell, and Ina Claire.

The Hard Way. 1943. Warner Brothers. Vincent Sherman, dir. With Ida Lupino and Joan Leslie.

Heat Lightning. 1934. Warner Brothers. Mervyn LeRoy, dir. With Aline Mac-Mahon and Ann Dvorak.

The House on 56th St. 1933. Warner Brothers. Robert Florey, dir. With Kay Francis and Gene Raymond.

I Found Stella Parish. 1935. Warner Brothers. Mervyn LeRoy, dir. With Kay Francis and Ian Hunter.

I'm No Angel. 1933. Paramount. Wesley Ruggles, dir. With Mae West and Cary Grant.

Imitation of Life. 1934. Universal. John Stahl, dir. With Claudette Colbert, Louise Beavers, and Warren Williams.

Impatient Maiden. 1932. Universal. James Whale, dir. With Mae Clark and Lew Ayres.

Indiscreet. 1931. United Artists. Leo McCarey, dir. With Gloria Swanson.

Jenny Gerhardt. 1935. Paramount. Marion Gering, dir. With Sylvia Sidney.

Kitty Foyle. 1940. RKO. Sam Wood, dir. With Ginger Rogers and James Craig.

Klondike Annie. 1936. Paramount. Raoul Walsh, dir. With Mae West.

Ladies of Leisure. 1930. Columbia. Frank Capra, dir. With Barbara Stanwyck.

Ladies of the Big House. 1932. Paramount. Marion Gering, dir. With Sylvia Sidney.

Ladies They Talk About. 1933. Warner Brothers. Howard Bretherton, dir. With Barbara Stanwyck and Preston Foster.

Letty Lynton. 1932. MGM. Clarence Brown, dir. With Joan Crawford, Robert Montgomery, and Nils Aster.

The Life of Vergie Winters. 1934. RKO. Alfred Santell, dir. With Ann Harding and John Boles.

Lilly Turner. 1933. Warner Brothers. William Wellman, dir. With Ruth Chatterton and George Brent.

Madame X. 1929. MGM. Lionel Barrymore, dir. With Ruth Chatterton.

Madame X. 1937. MGM. Sam Wood, dir. With Gladys George.

Mandalay. 1934. Warner Brothers. Michael Curtiz, dir. With Kay Francis and Ricardo Cortez.

Mannequin. 1937. MGM. Frank Borzage, dir. With Joan Crawford and Spencer Tracy.

A Man's Castle. 1933. Columbia. Frank Borzage, dir. With Loretta Young and Spencer Tracy.

Marked Woman. 1937. Warner Brothers. Lloyd Bacon, dir. With Bette Davis and Humphrey Bogart.

Mary Burns, Fugitive. 1935. Paramount. William Howard, dir. With Sylvia Sidney and Joan Bennett.

Mary Stevens, MD. 1933. Warner Brothers. Lloyd Bacon, dir. With Kay Francis and Lyle Talbot.

Millie. 1931. RKO. John Francis Dillon, dir. With Helen Twelvetrees.

The Miracle of Morgan's Creek. 1944. Paramount. Preston Sturges, dir. With Betty Hutton and Eddie Bracken.

My Favorite Wife. 1940. RKO. Garson Kanin, dir. With Irene Dunne and Cary Grant.

Nana. 1934. Goldwyn/United Artists. Dorothy Arzner, dir. With Anna Sten and Lionel Atwill.

Of Human Bondage. 1934. RKO. John Cromwell, dir. With Bette Davis and Leslie Howard.

The Old Maid. 1939. Warner Brothers. Edmund Goulding, dir. With Bette Davis and Miriam Hopkins.

Only Yesterday. 1933. Universal. John Stahl, dir. With Margaret Sullavan and John Boles.

Our Betters. 1933. RKO. George Cukor, dir. With Constance Bennett.

Our Dancing Daughters. 1928. MGM. Harry Beaumont, dir. With Joan Crawford, Dorothy Sebastian, and Anita Page.

Our Modern Maidens. 1929. MGM. Jack Conway, dir. With Joan Crawford and Anita Page.

Palm Beach Story. 1942. Paramount. Preston Sturges, dir. With Claudette Colbert and Joel McCrea.

Panama Flo. 1932. RKO. Ralph Murphy, dir. With Helen Twelvetrees and Charles Bickford.

Pick-Up. 1933. Paramount. Marion Gering, dir. With Sylvia Sidney.

Playing Around. 1930. Warner Brothers. Mervyn LeRoy, dir. With Alice White and Chester Morris.

Possessed. 1931. MGM. Clarence Brown, dir. With Joan Crawford and Clark Gable.

The Primrose Path. 1940. RKO. Gregory La Cava, dir. With Ginger Rogers and Joel McCrea.

Private Number. 1936. 20th Century-Fox. Roy Del Ruth, dir. With Loretta Young and Robert Taylor.

Red Dust. 1932. MGM. Victor Fleming, dir. With Clark Gable and Jean Harlow.

Red Headed Woman. 1932. MGM. Jack Conway, dir. With Jean Harlow and Chester Morris.

Rockabye. 1932. RKO. George Cukor, dir. With Constance Bennett and Joel McCrea.

Safe in Hell. 1931. Warner Brothers. William Wellman, dir. With Dorothy MacKaill and Donald Cook.

She Done Him Wrong. 1933. Paramount. Lowell Sherman, dir. With Mae West and Cary Grant.

She Had to Say Yes. 1933. Warner Brothers. Busby Berkeley, dir. With Loretta Young and Lyle Talbot.

Shopworn. 1932. Columbia. Nicholas Grinde, dir. With Barbara Stanwyck.

The Shopworn Angel. 1929. Paramount. Richard Wallace, dir. With Nancy Carroll, Gary Cooper, and Paul Lucas.

The Shopworn Angel. 1938. MGM. H. C. Potter, dir. With Margaret Sullavan, James Stewart, and Walter Pidgeon.

The Sin of Madelon Claudet. 1931. MGM. Edgar Selwyn, dir. With Helen Hayes and Neil Hamilton.

Stella Dallas. 1937. Goldwyn/United Artists. King Vidor, dir. With Barbara Stanwyck.

The Story of Temple Drake. 1933. Paramount. Stephen Roberts, dir. With Miriam Hopkins and Jack LaRue.

The Strange Love of Molly Louvain. 1932. Warner Brothers. Michael Curtiz, dir. With Ann Dvorak and Lee Tracy.

Strangers May Kiss. 1931. MGM. George Fitzmaurice, dir. With Norma Shearer.

Street of Women. 1932. Warner Brothers. Archie Mayo, dir. With Kay Francis and Roland Young.

Susan Lenox: Her Fall and Rise. 1931. MGM. Robert Z. Leonard, dir. With Greta Garbo and Clark Gable.

That Certain Woman. 1937. Warner Brothers. Edmund Goulding, dir. With Bette Davis, Ian Hunter, and Henry Fonda.

Three on a Match. 1932. Warner Brothers. Mervyn LeRoy, dir. With Joan Blondell, Ann Dvorak, and Bette Davis.

Torrid Zone. 1940. Warner Brothers. William Keighley, dir. With Ann Sheridan and James Cagney.

Two-Faced Woman. 1941. MGM. George Cukor, dir. With Greta Garbo and Melvyn Douglas.

Waterloo Bridge. 1931. Universal. James Whale, dir. With Mae Clark and Kent Douglas.

Waterloo Bridge. 1940. MGM. Mervyn LeRoy, dir. With Vivien Leigh and Robert Taylor.

White Cargo. 1942. 20th Century-Fox. Richard Thorpe, dir. With Hedy Lamarr and Walter Pidgeon.

NOTES

Preface

1. On the criticism of Stahl's 1932 script see the three undated memos from Lamar Trotti to Jason Joy and Joy's letter to Carl Laemmle, March 4, 1932; for a reference to the Legion's objections and the decision to remake the film see Joseph Breen, Memo, February 1, 1938, and I. Auster, Memo, March 23, 1939, *Back Street*, MPPDA Case Files, Special Collections, Academy Library.

1. The Fallen Woman Film and the Impetus for Censorship

1. Jason Joy to Harry Cohn, January 16, 1932, *Shopworn*, MPPDA Case Files, Academy Library.

2. For a recent instance of this argument see Leonard J. Leff and Jerold L. Simmons, *The Dame in the Kimono: Hollywood, Censorship, and the Production Code from the 1920s to the 1960s* (New York: Grove Weidenfeld, 1990), 19–32.

3. Robert Sklar, *Movie-Made America: How the Movies Changed American Life* (New York: Random House, 1975), 74–76, discusses this news story in connection with the star scandals of the teens; the phrase "movie struck girl" derives from William A. Page, "The Movie Struck Girl," *Women's Home Companion* 45 (June 1918): 18, cited in Sklar.

4. These examples are culled from a random selection of issues from the early thirties: Roland Francis, "The New Extra Girl," *Photoplay* (December 1929): 44–45, 122; Reginald Taviner, "Is It Easy Money?" *Photoplay* (March 1931): 52–53, 123–25; Jeanne North, "Do You Want a Job in the Studios?" *Photoplay* (May 1931): 68–70, 116–20; for a short story dealing with the same themes see Vesta Wills Hancock, "Ambitious Baby," *Photoplay* (May 1930): 58–59, 152–55.

5. Will Hays, *Memoirs* (New York: Doubleday, 1955), 380.

6. For references to the gangster film and the fantasy of being a criminal, see Herbert Blumer and Philip M. Hauser, *Movies, Delinquency, and Crime* (New York: Macmillan, 1933), 2, 46–59. In discussing the influence of movies on delinquent girls, Blumer and Hauser do not use the term "sex picture" (the

163

term is employed in industry journals such as *Variety*), but cf. the discussion of the representation of a "wild life" outside of the context of the family (87); the reference to the figure of the gold digger (100); and the discussion of films in which the sexually deviant heroine is "punished" by disease, illegitimate children, and social ostracism (117). I discuss the model of spectatorship inherent in the Payne Fund Studies in "Reformers and Spectators: The Film Education Movement in the Thirties," *Camera Obscura* 22 (Jan. 1990): 29–49.

7. Blumer and Hauser, *Movies, Delinquency, and Crime* 208.

8. Please see the objections to the fallen woman film, 15–17.

9. Film critics have proposed several names for this type of film: the confession tale (Richard Griffith), the maternal melodrama (Christian Viviani), and the fallen woman cycle (Marilyn Campbell, Betsy McLane). See Marilyn Campbell, "RKO's Fallen Women, 1930–1933," *Velvet Light Trap* 10 (Fall 1973): 13–16; Richard Griffith, "Cycles and Genres," from "The Film Since Then," an additional section of the book *The Film Till Now* by Paul Rotha (London: Vision Press, 1949); Betsy Ann McLane, "Hollywood's Fallen Women Features," Masters Thesis, University of Southern California, 1978; Christian Viviani, "Who Is without Sin?: The Maternal Melodrama in American Film, 1930–1939," *Wide Angle* 4, no. 2 (1980): 4–17. I have decided to retain the name fallen woman cycle in order to emphasize the continuities between the films and their literary antecedents.

10. Review of *Madame X, Variety*, May 1, 1929.

11. The trilogy, which has probably been mistitled *Past and Present*, is discussed in Nina Auerbach, *Woman and the Demon: The Life of a Victorian Myth* (Cambridge: Harvard University Press, 1982), 154–59; Linda Nochlin, "Lost and *Found:* Once More the Fallen Woman," *Art Bulletin* 60 (1978): 141–44; Raymond Lister, *Victorian Narrative Painting* (New York: C. N. Potter, 1966), 54–59.

12. Linda Nochlin, ("Lost and *Found*") discusses this icon in connection with George Frederic Watts's *Found Drowned* (c. 1848–50), in which the fallen woman's body appears under the arch of a bridge.

13. For an interesting discussion of the woman's seduction/rape by an upper-class man as a figuration of class conflict, see Thomas Elsaesser, "Tales of Sound and Fury: Observations on the Family Melodrama," *Monogram* 4 (1972), reprinted in *Home Is Where the Heart Is: Studies in Melodrama and the Woman's Film*, ed. Christine Gledhill (London: British Film Institute, 1987), 45–46.

14. Sally Mitchell, *The Fallen Angel: Chastity, Class, and Women's Reading, 1835–1880* (Bowling Green, Ohio: Bowling Green University Popular Press, 1981); George Watt, *The Fallen Woman in the Nineteenth-Century Novel* (Totowa, N.J.: Barnes and Noble, 1984).

15. See Mitchell, *Fallen Angel* 8.

16. Nina Baym, *Women's Fiction: A Guide to Novels by and about Women in America, 1820–1870* (Ithaca: Cornell University Press, 1978), 51. Baym claims that relatively few American domestic novels represent women as the sexual prey of men (26), but she does not take account of the fact that British domestic novels, among them fallen woman stories, were widely read in America. See Dee Garrison, "Immoral Fiction in the Late Victorian Library," *American Quarterly* 28, no. 1 (Spring 1976): 74.

17. Sally Mitchell, Introduction, *East Lynne* (New Brunswick, N.J.: Rutgers University Press, 1984), vii and xiii.

18. Anne Lyon Haight, *Banned Books: 387 B.C. to 1978 A.D.*, updated and enlarged by Chandler B. Grannis (New York: R. R. Bowker, 1978), 55.

19. Mrs. Gaskell was troubled by the reaction to *Ruth*, one of the first sympathetic depictions of the fallen woman. In one of her letters she notes: "in several instances I have *forbidden* people to write, for their expressions of disapproval (although I have known that the feeling would exist in them,) would be very painful and stinging at the time. 'An unfit subject or fiction' is *the* thing to say about it . . . 'Deep regret' is what my friends here . . . feel and express." See Elizabeth Gaskell to Anne Robson, before January 27, 1853, *The Letters of Mrs. Gaskell*, ed. J. A. V. Chapple and Arthur Pollard (Manchester: Manchester University Press, 1966), 220, quoted in Mitchell, *Fallen Angel* 40. Like *Ruth*, Frances Trollope's novel *Jessie Phillips* provoked a great deal of complaint, leading the author to complain of receiving "such a multitude of communications urging various and contradictory modes of treating the subject." See Frances Trollope, *Jessie Phillips: A Tale of the Present Day* (London: Colburn, 1844), chap. 56, quoted in Mitchell, *Fallen Angel* 25.

20. Haight, *Banned Books* 40, 45, 51. Sally Mitchell notes that in order to be published in book form, several magazine serials dealing with the fallen woman had to be revised to meet the requirements of publishers and circulating libraries (*Fallen Angel* 88–89).

21. Dominick LaCapra, *Madame Bovary on Trial* (Ithaca: Cornell University Press, 1982).

22. Ernest Boyd, Introduction to the Modern Library Edition of *Nana* (New York: Random House, 1928), v–vi.

23. On the question of sexual practices outside the dictates of the ideology of purity see Michel Foucault, *The History of Sexuality*, vol. 1: *An Introduction*, trans. Robert Hurley (New York: Vintage Books, 1978); Peter Gay, *Education of the Senses*, vol. 1 of *The Bourgeois Experience: Victoria to Freud* (Oxford: Oxford University Press, 1984). On the feminine ideal see Barbara Welter, "The Cult of True Womanhood: 1820–1860," *American Quarterly* 18 (Summer 1966): 151–74; Mitchell, *Fallen Angel* x–xvi; and Nancy F. Cott, "Passionlessness: An Interpretation of Victorian Sexual Ideology, 1790–1850," *Signs* 4, no. 2 (Winter 1978): 219–36.

24. Haight, *Banned Books* 53.

25. George Bernard Shaw, Preface to *Mrs. Warren's Profession,* in *Bernard Shaw: Collected Plays with Their Prefaces,* vol. 1 (New York: Dodd, Mead, 1975), 231–32.

26. Dreiser's difficulties with his publisher, Doubleday, Page and Company, are discussed by John C. Berkey and Alice M. Winters in the "Historical Commentary" to *Sister Carrie* (Philadelphia: University of Pennsylvania Press, 1981).

27. Elizabeth Janeway, Afterword, *Susan Lenox: Her Fall and Rise* (Carbondale: Southern Illinois University Press, 1977), xviii.

28. David Graham Phillips, *Susan Lenox: Her Fall and Rise* 150.

29. John S. Sumner, Anthony Comstock's successor as head of the New York Society for the Suppression of Vice, attempted to dissuade D. Appleton from publishing the book. See Haight, *Banned Books* 59; Janeway, Afterword xi–xii.

30. Haight, *Banned Books* 27.

31. The Formula is reprinted in Garth Jowett, *Film: The Democratic Art* (Boston: Little, Brown, 1976), 466–67.

32. The Code is reprinted in Raymond Moley, *The Hays Office* (New York: Bobbs Merrill, 1945), 241–48, and a somewhat shorter version appears in Jowett, *Film* 468–72.

33. While I discuss only American fallen woman films, there are also many European variants of the story. For example, in the Italian diva film *Lydia* (tentatively dated 1910 by the Cineteca Italiana), the heroine runs off with a wealthy nobleman, an act which precipitates her ailing mother's death and leads to public disgrace, and eventually death, for her lover and herself. Many Asta Nielsen films of the same period deal with the fallen woman, including *Afgrunden* (1910), *Heisses Blut* (1911), *Im grossen Augenblick* (1911), *Die arme Jenny* (1912), and *Die Sünden der Väter* (1913). Nielsen's films are described in *Asta Nielsen: Ihr Leben in Fotodokumenten, Selbstzeugnissen und zeitgenössischen Betrachtungen,* ed. Renate Seydel and Allan Hagedorff (Munich: Universitas Verlag, 1981). The German "street" films of the twenties are also a prime example of the genre, most notably *Die freudlose Gasse.* Patrice Petro discusses the German variants of the genre in "*Dirnentragödie:* Sexual Mobility, Social Mobility, and Melodramas of the Street," in her *Joyless Streets: Women and Melodramatic Representation in Weimar Germany* (Princeton: Princeton University Press, 1989), 160–74.

34. For examples, see the review of *It* in *Variety* (February 9, 1927) and Harry Edington, Letter to George J. Schaefer, August 15, 1940, *Kitty Foyle,* RKO Production Files, RKO Archive, Los Angeles.

35. Griffith, "Cycles and Genres," 438–39; and see McLane, "Hollywood's Fallen Women Features," 206–7.

36. Viviani, "Who Is without Sin?"

37. William Troy, "Virtue in 1933," in a weekly column "Films," *Nation*, March 29, 1933, 354–55.

38. Edgar Dale, *The Content of Motion Pictures* (New York: Macmillan, 1935), 108.

39. Ibid., 107.

40. Alice Ames Winter to Will Hays, July 10, 1933, Hays Collection, Indiana State Library.

41. *Photoplay*, September 1931, cited in Campbell, "RKO's Fallen Women."

42. Mildred Martin, of the *Philadelphia Inquirer*, July 23, 1933, as quoted in a public relations report to Will Hays from K. L. Russell, July 26, 1933, Hays Collection, Indiana State Library.

43. Blumer and Hauser, *Movies, Delinquency, and Crime* 96.

44. Ibid., 42.

45. Jason Joy to William A. Orr, June 14, 1932, *Red Headed Woman*, MPPDA Case Files, Academy Library.

46. James Wingate to Will Hays, n.d., *Jennie Gerhardt*, MPPDA Case Files, Academy Library.

47. Moley, *Hays Office* 77–82.

48. Not surprisingly, Moley, in what amounts to a celebration of Hays and the wonders of industry self-regulation, does not emphasize the majors' oligopolistic control of the first-run exhibition outlets. For a discussion of the significance of theater ownership see Mae D. Huettig, *Economic Control of the Motion Picture Industry: A Study in Industrial Organization* (Philadelphia: University of Pennsylvania Press, 1944).

49. Jack Vizzard, *See No Evil: Life inside a Hollywood Censor* (New York: Simon & Schuster, Pocket Book Edition, 1971); James M. Wall, "Oral History with Geoffrey Shurlock," Louis B. Mayer Library, American Film Institute, Los Angeles (A.F.I., 1975).

50. Wall, "Oral History with Geoffrey Shurlock," 254–300.

51. I have run across one case in which the MPPDA sought to block the exhibition of a film, the 1929 version of *White Cargo*. The film was produced in Britain by an independent, J. B. Williams, who was not a member of the association. Significantly, the 1942 version, made by 20th Century-Fox, was released with MPPDA approval.

52. Vizzard, *See No Evil* 63. Shurlock also mentions the importance of reviewing scripts prior to production in Wall, "Oral History with Geoffrey Shurlock," 126: "As usual in those days they had to take it [problematic material] out of the script before anything lurid could be even conceived. It was our policy to question everything, to be sure we had a basis to raise questions later on; we didn't want him [the producer?] asking us afterward: 'Why didn't you tell me at the script level?' "

53. Discussing the MPPDA's pledge to "enforce" the Code in 1934, Sklar writes: "The movie producers already possessed a code of moral standards, the Production Code of 1930, which went about as far as it could toward expressing the Catholic bishops' viewpoint without converting the movies from entertainment to popular theology" (*Movie-Made America*, 173). Garth Jowett writes: "by 1935 the motion picture industry was essentially under the control of a Catholic hegemony" (*Film*, 256).

54. The Legion printed ratings of current releases and circulated these among its members. "C" (Condemned) films were "considered to be those which, because of theme or treatment, have been described by the Holy Father as 'positively bad' " ("Explanation of Film Classifications," National Catholic Office for Motion Pictures, undated pamphlet held by the Library of Performing Arts, New York Public Library, New York). Shurlock discusses the case of Lubitsch's *Two-Faced Woman* which was condemned by the Legion; see Wall, "Oral History with Geoffrey Shurlock," 249–50. A listing of films classified by the Legion shows a somewhat larger number of films given a "B" (Objectionable in part, for all) rather than an outright "C" rating. Examples are *Kitty Foyle*, *Forever Amber*, *The Gay Sisters*, and *Dance, Girls, Dance*. See the fascinating "Motion Pictures Classified by the National Legion of Decency, February 1936–November 1948," undated pamphlet held in the Library of Performing Arts, New York Public Library.

55. Annette Kuhn has also analyzed film censorship as a constructive force in the elaboration of meaning. See the essay on the Production Code and Howard Hawks's *The Big Sleep* in *The Power of the Image: Essays on Representation and Sexuality* (London: Routledge & Kegan Paul, 1985), 74–95, and, on British cinema, *Cinema, Censorship, and Sexuality 1909–1925* (London: Routledge, 1988).

56. This approach toward the relationship between film and ideology is proposed by Jean-Louis Comolli and Jean Narboni, "Cinema/Ideology/Criticism," *Cahiers du Cinéma* (Oct/Nov 1969), translated in *Screen* 12, no. 1 (Spring 1971): 27–36. The *Cahiers* produced two collective texts on film which, they argued, revealed the contradictions within ideology. See "John Ford's *Young Mr. Lincoln*" (July/Aug 1970), translated in *Screen* 13, no. 3 (Autumn 1972), reprinted in *Movies and Methods*, vol. 1, ed. Bill Nichols (Berkeley: University of California Press, 1976), and *"Morocco"* (Nov/Dec 1970), translated in *Sternberg*, ed. Peter Baxter (London: BFI Publishing, 1980).

57. See, for example, Claire Johnston, "Woman's Cinema as Counter-Cinema," in *Notes on Women's Cinema*, BFI pamphlet (London: 1973), reprinted in *Movies and Methods*, vol. 1, ed. Bill Nichols (Berkeley: University of California Press, 1976). For a critique of Johnston's methods of analysis see Janet Bergstrom, "Rereading the Work of Claire Johnston," *Camera Obscura* 3/4 (1979): 21–32.

58. Richard Maltby, " 'Baby Face' or How Joe Breen Made Barbara Stanwyck Atone for Causing the Wall Street Crash," *Screen* 27, no. 2 (March/April 1986): 24. Barbara Klinger also finds the category of the subversive text problematic, suggesting that it is necessary to take account of the multiplicity of discourses which determine the consumption of the supposedly subversive or progressive text, see "Cinema/Ideology/Criticism Revisited: The Progressive Text," *Screen* 25, no. 1 (Jan/Feb 1984): 44.

59. On April 4, 1928, Jason Joy writes to Will Hays from the West Coast, announcing that he has secured furniture for the establishment of an office, Letter, Hays Collection, Indiana State Library. I suspect that the establishment of censorship on the West Coast was in response to the coming of sound. The relationship between the Bureau of Motion Pictures and the MPPDA in the forties is discussed in Clayton R. Koppes and Gregory D. Black, *Hollywood Goes to War: How Politics, Profits, and Propaganda Shaped World War II Movies* (New York: Macmillan, 1987), 82–112.

2. The Studio Relations Committee's Policies and Procedures

1. For a discussion of the role of the star scandals in the formation of the MPPDA see Richard de Cordova, "The Emergence of the Star System in America: An Examination of the Institutional and Ideological Function of the Star, 1907–1922," Diss., University of California-Los Angeles, 1986, 250–70. For a description of the MPPDA's public relations department see Herbert Shenton, *The Public Relations of the Motion Picture Industry* (1931; rpt. New York: Jerome S. Ozer, 1971); an interesting analysis of Hays's public relations policies in the twenties may be found in Ruth A. Inglis, *Freedom of the Movies: A Report from the Commission on Freedom of the Press* (Chicago: University of Chicago Press, 1947), 105–11.

2. Kristin Thompson, *Exporting Entertainment: America in the World Film Market, 1907–1934* (London: British Film Institute, 1985), 117–24.

3. Hays's explanation of the import of these policies is somewhat different from the one presented here; see his *Memoirs*, 335–57.

4. Michael Conant, *Antitrust in the Motion Picture Industry* (Berkeley: University of California Press, 1960), 202–3.

5. See Memo, Fred Beetson to Hays, May 4, 1926, and the unsigned Confidential Report of January 31, 1927, Hays Collection, Indiana State Library.

6. Throughout the late twenties and early thirties, the acquisition of literary properties by the studios was cleared through McKenzie's office in New York. For example, see Jason Joy's letters to McKenzie, dated April 16, 1928, and March 12, 1930, on Columbia's acquisition of the play *Ladies of the Evening*,

Ladies of Leisure, MPPDA Case Files, Academy Library. In this period, McKenzie's office played a large part in the preparation of scripts from controversial novels such as William Faulkner's *Sanctuary* and Theodore Dreiser's *An American Tragedy*; see *The Story of Temple Drake* and *An American Tragedy*, MPPDA Case Files, Academy Library.

7. Jowett describes the origins of the "Don'ts and Be Carefuls" (*Film* 238–40) and characterizes the procedures for reviewing films as "informal" in this period (237).

8. As previously noted, Jason Joy wrote to Will Hays from the West Coast, announcing that he had secured furniture for the establishment of an office for reviewing scripts, Joy to Hays, April 4, 1928, Hays Collection, Indiana State Library. Joy's correspondence with Hays indicates that during 1928 he performed two other sorts of tasks: he consulted with Fred Beetson who was handling labor disputes within the studios, and he did public relations work with women's organizations; see the letters dated April 6, 1928, April 21, 1928, and May 19, 1928, Hays Collection, Indiana State Library.

9. In the case of *Possessed* (MGM, 1931) Joy notes: "The philosophy of this one is wrong. For some reason we did not have the script and did not get in a crack before the picture was finished. This cannot happen again and was the chief reason the Code was amended making submission of scripts mandatory. . . ." Joy to Joseph Breen, Dec. 15, 1931, *Possessed*, MPPDA Case Files, Academy Library. Within my sample of fallen woman films, large numbers of case files survive for films after 1930, lending credence to the claim that the submission of scripts to Joy's office had become routine by this time.

10. Jason Joy to Hays, October 3, 1932, Hays Collection, Indiana State Library. Joy writes: "You will have in mind that the time of the head of this office is largely devoted to consultations with the heads of studios concerning stories to be put into production and with the various members of his staff in the office concerning the particular scripts and pictures assigned to them. The head of the department is out of the office a large part of every day and at irregular intervals."

11. Jason Joy to Hays, April 4, 1928, Hays Collection, Indiana State Library.

12. This is the date of a letter in which Joy mentions his work for the Studio Relations Committee, *Safe in Hell*, MPPDA Case Files, Academy Library.

13. *Red Headed Woman*, MPPDA Case Files, Academy Library.

14. James Wingate to Hays, March 21, 1933, Hays Collection, Indiana State Library.

15. MPPDA, Publicity Release for Morning Papers, September 15, 1932, Hays Collection, Indiana State Library.

16. Joy to Hays, October 3, 1932, Hays Collection, Indiana State Library.

17. Breen to James Wingate, March 5, 1933, *Ann Vickers*, MPPDA Case Files, Academy Library.

18. Memo, Maurice McKenzie to Breen, August 10, 1933, *A Man's Castle*, MPPDA Case Files, Academy Library.

19. Breen to Wingate, March 17, 1933, *The Story of Temple Drake*, MPPDA Case Files, and Breen to Will Hays, June 8, 1933, *Baby Face*, MPPDA Case Files, Academy Library.

20. Jowett, *Film* 170–71.

21. This group was established in 1925 under the direction of the Reverend Charles Scanlon, general director of the Department of Moral Welfare of the U.S. Presbyterian Church. Later, it was under the direction of the Reverend William Sheaf Chase, in association with Miss Maude M. Aldrich, National Motion Picture Chairman of the Women's Christian Temperance Union, Mrs. Robbins Gilman of the Women's Cooperative Alliance of Minneapolis, and the Reverend Clifford B. Twombly. See Shenton, *Public Relations of the Motion Picture Industry* 106–11.

22. According to Jowett, *Film* 170, the Upshaw Bill of 1926 proposed the formation of a federal censorship board; the Hudson Bill (HR 9986) of 1930 proposed a censorship board and would have outlawed the marketing practices of blockbooking and blindselling; the Brookhart Bill (S1003) was concerned with economic regulation of the industry.

23. Ira Carmen, *Movies, Censorship, and the Law* (Ann Arbor: University of Michigan Press, 1967), 129.

24. Hays writes that the Studio Relations Committee personnel "ought to be able to gauge . . . the possible censorship reaction to any picture which they have seen and worked on," Hays to Jason Joy, November 18, 1933, *A Man's Castle*, MPPDA Case Files, Academy Library. Also, a memo discussing possible replacements for Jason Joy notes that Joy's strengths lie in his knowledge of "previous reactions of censor boards [and] facility in suggesting variations of treatment to overcome code or censor worries," C. E. M. [Carl Milliken?] to Hays, June 25, 1932, Hays Collection, Indiana State Library.

25. James M. Wall, "Oral History with Geoffrey Shurlock," 209.

26. Moley, *Hays Office* 68–76.

27. Wall, "Oral History with Geoffrey Shurlock," 255.

28. James Wingate to Adolph Zukor, n.d., *The Story of Temple Drake*, MPPDA Case Files, Academy Library.

29. Taken from the version of the Code given in Moley, *Hays Office* 244.

30. See for example Raymond Bellour "Segmenter/Analyser" in *L'analyse du film* (Paris: Editions Albatros, 1979), 247–70.

31. Prints were not available to me for six of the one hundred films in my sample: *Call Her Savage, The Easiest Way, East Is West*, the two versions of *The Shopworn Angel*, and *Strangers May Kiss* (please see Censorship Cases Reviewed, 157–62). I have retained these films in the sample because the MPPDA files in and of themselves are of great interest.

32. H. G. Nathanson, Regal Films Ltd, to W. D. Kelly, MGM, May 4, 1931, *The Easiest Way*, MPPDA Case Files, Academy Library.

33. According to the *New York Times* (March 29, 1911), the mayor of Boston cut short the run of the play. The play was also considered scandalous in England; see "London 'Boos' for 'The Easiest Way,' " *New York Times*, February 11, 1912. I am indebted to Tom Gunning for this reference. The film version I discuss was preceded by Lewis Selznick's 1917 version, mentioned in the MPPDA correspondence by Joy in a telegram to M. M. (probably Maurice McKenzie), October 3, 1928, *The Easiest Way*, MPPDA Case Files, Academy Library.

34. The first complete draft of the script, by Edith Ellis, is dated October 28, 1930, *The Easiest Way*, MGM Story Files, Special Collections, USC.

35. John Wilson, Memo, n.d., *The Easiest Way*, MPPDA Case Files, Academy Library.

36. The MGM Story File, Special Collections, USC, contains various permutations of the ending by Edith Ellis and Kenyon Nicholson.

37. Joy to Irving Thalberg, *The Easiest Way*, MPPDA Case Files, Academy Library.

38. *The Easiest Way*, MGM Story Files, Special Collections, USC.

39. Joy to Thalberg, November 10, 1930, *The Easiest Way*, MPPDA Case Files, Academy Library.

40. First Complete Draft by Edith Ellis, October 28, 1930, p. 49, *The Easiest Way*, MGM Story Files, Special Collections, USC.

41. Cutting Continuity Script (final version), December 31, 1930, *The Easiest Way*, MGM Story Files, Special Collections, USC.

42. First Complete Draft, p. 52, *The Easiest Way*.

43. Joy to Thalberg, December 18, 1930, *The Easiest Way*, MPPDA Case Files, Academy Library.

44. James Wingate to Jason Joy, February 11, 1931, *The Easiest Way*, MPPDA Case Files, Academy Library.

45. Joy to Thalberg, November 10, 1930, *The Easiest Way*, MPPDA Case Files, Academy Library.

46. John Wilson, Memo, n.d., *The Easiest Way*, MPPDA Case Files, Academy Library.

47. One ending is given in Joy's letter of November 10, 1930, and the second in the memo by John Wilson, *The Easiest Way*, MPPDA Case Files, Academy Library.

48. This ending is written by Kenyon Nicholson; see the "Miscellaneous Dialogue" dated December 9, 1930, and the fragment of the script dated December 2, 1930, in *The Easiest Way*, MGM Story Files, Special Collections, USC.

49. Joy to Thalberg, December 18, 1930, *The Easiest Way*, MPPDA Case Files, Academy Library.

50. H. G. Nathanson, Regal Films Ltd., to W. D. Kelly, MGM, May 4, 1931, *The Easiest Way*, MPPDA Case Files, Academy Library.

51. Lamar Trotti, who was working in the New York office at this point, writes to Joy concerning negotiations he conducted with Wingate. He asks for a clarification of policy: "If it is the understanding of the Association that I personally or someone here is to attempt to change the attitudes of the boards and to make a fight on every picture which is released . . ." Trotti to Joy, February 21, 1931, *The Easiest Way*, MPPDA Case Files, Academy Library.

52. Joy to Wingate, February 5, 1931, *The Easiest Way*, MPPDA Case Files, Academy Library.

53. Wingate to Joy, February 11, 1931, *The Easiest Way*, MPPDA Case Files, Academy Library.

3. *Glamour and Gold Diggers*

1. Emile Zola, *Nana*, Modern Library Edition (New York: Random House, 1927), 357.

2. See Kristin Thompson, "Settings and Depth," in David Bordwell, Janet Staiger, and Kristin Thompson, *The Classical Hollywood Cinema: Film Style and Mode of Production to 1960* (New York: Columbia University Press, 1985), 216–21.

3. John Hambley and Patrick Downing, *The Art of Hollywood: A Thames Television Exhibition at the Victoria and Albert Museum* (London: Macdermott & Chant, 1979), 62.

4. Ibid., 54.

5. Ibid., 61–62.

6. Cited in ibid., 61.

7. Secretary's Report for Review Committee, National Board of Review, n.d., *Our Modern Maidens*, MPPDA Case Files, Academy Library.

8. Warner Brothers Press Books, United Artists Collection, State Historical Society, Madison, Wisconsin.

9. The streamlined moderne style of interior design is generally taken to be the thirties variant of art deco. While there are important formal distinctions to be made between the two, both styles were a product of what David Gebhard calls a "commercial vernacular." Borrowed from sources as disparate as cubism, Mayan architecture, and the Bauhaus school of design, the motifs of art deco and later moderne were applied to a wide variety of mass-produced artifacts—from tricycles to lipstick cases—and began to dominate graphic design in advertising. On the distinction between deco and moderne see David Gebhard, "The Moderne in the U.S., 1920–1941," *Architectural Association Quarterly* 2 (1970): 6–7; Bevis Hillier, *The World of Art Deco*, catalogue for an exhibition organized by the Minneapolis Institute of the Arts (New York: E. P.

Dutton, 1971), 23–25; on design as a marketing strategy see Adrian Forty, *Objects of Desire: Design and Society from Wedgwood to IBM* (New York: Pantheon, 1986), 90–91.

10. Donald Albrecht, *Designing Dreams: Modern Architecture in the Movies* (New York: Harper & Row, 1986), 95.

11. Ibid., 111.

12. Howard Mandelbaum and Eric Myers, *Screen Deco: A Celebration of High Style in Hollywood* (New York: St. Martin's Press, 1985), 13.

13. Lary May, *Screening Out the Past: The Birth of Mass Culture and the Motion Picture Industry* (Oxford: Oxford University Press, 1980), 232–36.

14. Charles Eckert, "The Carole Lombard in Macy's Window," *Quarterly Review of Film Studies* 3, no. 1 (Winter 1978): 1–21.

15. First Complete Draft, p. 52, *The Easiest Way*, MGM Story Files, Special Collections, USC.

16. Eckert, "Carole Lombard in Macy's Window," 8.

17. Lamar Trotti, Memo, September 29, 1930, *The Greeks Had a Word for Them*, MPPDA Case Files, Academy Library.

18. Telegram, Hays to Jack Wilson, June 12, 1931; a résumé, November 14, 1931, notes Hays saw a preview with Joy, Trotti, and Wilson; a résumé, November 18, 1931, notes further changes were requested; a résumé, November 25, 1931, notes Hays and Breen saw an altered print, *The Greeks Had a Word for Them*, MPPDA Case Files, Academy Library.

19. Trotti to Samuel Goldwyn, August 18, 1931, *The Greeks Had a Word for Them*, MPPDA Case Files, Academy Library.

20. Warner Brothers Press Books, United Artists Collection, State Historical Society, Madison, Wisconsin.

21. Lamar Trotti writes: "We suggest that you clean up the character of Polaire, who is the sympathy character of the play. It would be well not only to have her marry Dey, as she does now, but to establish, if possible, that she is not of the same character as the other girls, although she is on friendly terms with them," Trotti to Goldwyn, August 18, 1931, *The Greeks Had a Word for Them*, MPPDA Case Files, Academy Library.

22. For an account of the industry's regulation of advertising posters see Mary Beth Haralovich, "Motion Picture Advertising: Industrial and Social Forces and Effects," Diss., University of Wisconsin–Madison, 1984.

23. External reform groups frequently complained about West's wisecracks, and industry censors were led to negotiate with the studio at some length over particular lines. For example, the line "You can be had" is discussed in the correspondence between James Wingate and Harold Hurley, Letters of November 9 and 29, 1932, *She Done Him Wrong*, MPPDA Case Files, Academy Library.

24. Alice Ames Winter to Will Hays, July 10, 1933, Hays Collection, Indiana State Library.

25. Mrs. Alonzo Richardson, Better Films Society of Atlanta, to Carl Milliken, *Red Headed Woman*, MPPDA Case Files, Academy Library.

26. Public relations report to Will Hays from K. L. Russell, November 17, 1933, Hays Collection, Indiana State Library.

27. Sidney Kent to Will Hays, n.d., *She Done Him Wrong*, MPPDA Case Files, Academy Library.

28. Breen to Hays, October 7, 1935, *She Done Him Wrong*, MPPDA Case Files, Academy Library.

29. MGM's distribution agent discusses his difficulties with the Canadian board in an unsigned letter to H. Cass, Regal Films, Toronto, *Red Headed Woman*, MPPDA Case Files, Academy Library.

30. On RKO's negotiations with the British censor board see Memo, Margot Fragey to Pandro Berman, August 16, 1933, and the unsigned letter to Ned Depinet, August 25, 1933, RKO Legal Files, RKO Studio Archive, Los Angeles.

31. Lists of cuts may be found in the MPPDA Case Files for *Red Headed Woman*, *Bed of Roses*, and *She Done Him Wrong*, Academy Library.

32. Martin Quigley, *Decency in Motion Pictures* (New York: Macmillan, 1937), 32–33; information on the film's reception by the boards is given in the reports on state censorship in *Baby Face*, MPPDA Case Files, Academy Library.

33. Wingate to Darryl Zanuck, January 3, 1933, *Baby Face*, MPPDA Case Files, Academy Library.

34. While there are various treatments, there is only one basic version of the script. All references here are to the "Master Final" dated December 17, 1932, *Baby Face*, Warners Story File, Special Collections, USC.

35. Maltby, " 'Baby Face' or How Joe Breen Made Barbara Stanwyck Atone for Causing the Wall Street Crash," 22–45. Maltby explains the censorship of this film as a reaction to the way in which it thematizes the moral and economic excesses of the nineteen twenties. While I would agree that the Depression figures as a theme in this film, I think class rise, rather than the idea of waste or economic ruin, is what destabilizes the representation of female sexuality. *Baby Face* resembles other examples of the cycle in that class rise motivates the gold digger's aggressivity and makes her a threatening figure.

36. Wingate to Zanuck, January 3, 1933, and Report to Hays, n.d., *Baby Face*, MPPDA Case Files, Academy Library.

37. The "tag" is simply added to the Master Final Script, *Baby Face*, Warners Story Files, Special Collections, USC.

38. Will Hays, Memo, April 20, 1933, *Baby Face*, MPPDA Case Files, Academy Library.

39. Wingate to Zanuck, January 3, 1933, *Baby Face*, MPPDA Case Files, Academy Library.

40. Wingate to Zanuck, February 28, 1933, *Baby Face*, MPPDA Case Files, Academy Library.

41. Wingate to Hays, May 30, 1933, *Baby Face*, MPPDA Case Files, Academy Library.

42. Wingate to Zanuck, February 28, 1933, *Baby Face*, MPPDA Case Files, Academy Library.

43. Jason Joy to B. P. Schulberg, November 17, 1931, *One Hour with You*, MPPDA Case Files, Academy Library.

44. Joy to Harold Hurley, July 21, 1932, *Trouble in Paradise*, MPPDA Case Files, Academy Library.

45. Wingate to Jack Warner, May 11, 1933, *Baby Face*, MPPDA Case Files, Academy Library.

46. Hays, Memo of April 20, 1933, *Baby Face*, MPPDA Case Files, Academy Library.

47. Wingate to Jack Warner, April 26, 1933, *Baby Face*, MPPDA Case Files, Academy Library.

48. Wingate to Jack Warner, May 11, 1933, *Baby Face*, MPPDA Case Files, Academy Library.

49. Lamar Trotti to Will Hays, June 9, 1931, *The Greeks Had a Word for Them*, MPPDA Case Files, Academy Library. Trotti notes that the three girls going off on the boat with the aviators is contrary to the Code and suggests: "For picture purposes it would seem better to bring Polaire and her young man together and let them go away to be married, leaving the future of the other girls somewhat in doubt, if desirable."

50. Joy to Carl Milliken, July 7, 1932, *Red Headed Woman*, MPPDA Case Files, Academy Library. Samuel Goldwyn apparently took a similar position on *The Greeks Had a Word for Them*. Lamar Trotti writes to Jason Joy: "I think they realize that they have quite a tough proposition, but of course Sam takes the position he took before, that he had to make it and that as it's a comedy, it's all right," Trotti to Joy, October 29, 1931, *The Greeks Had a Word for Them*, MPPDA Case Files, Academy Library.

51. Wingate to Will Hays, December 2, 1932, *She Done Him Wrong*, MPPDA Case Files, Academy Library.

52. Unsigned Letter to H. Cass, Regal Films, Toronto, *Red Headed Woman*, MPPDA Case Files, Academy Library.

53. Breen makes reference to this clause of the Code in a review of *The Greeks Had a Word for Them*, in one of his first memos, unsigned and dated November 30, 1931, *The Greeks Had a Word for Them*, MPPDA Case Files, Academy Library.

4. Something Other than a Sob Story

1. E. Ann Kaplan, *Women and Film: Both Sides of the Camera* (New York: Methuen, 1983), 49–60. Kaplan develops her view of the maternal melodrama

in "Mothering, Feminism, and Representation: The Maternal in Melodrama and the Woman's Film, 1910–40," in *Home Is Where the Heart Is: Studies in Melodrama and the Woman's Film,* ed. Christine Gledhill (London: British Film Institute, 1987), 113–37.

2. Linda Williams, " 'Something Else besides a Mother': *Stella Dallas* and the Maternal Melodrama," *Cinema Journal* 24, no. 1 (Fall 1984): 2–27.

3. Mrs. Clifton Perkins and Mrs. I. V. Gowing to MPPDA, November 2, 1931, *The Sin of Madelon Claudet,* MPPDA Case Files, Academy Library.

4. Preview by Maude Lathem, at the Academy, December 2, 1932, *Rockabye,* MPPDA Case Files, Academy Library.

5. Joseph von Sternberg, *Fun in a Chinese Laundry* (New York: Macmillan, 1965), 264.

6. This analysis relies principally on three versions of the script, dated March 18, April 23, and May 11, 1932, in *Blonde Venus,* Paramount Story Files, Academy Library. There are two other versions, dated August 31 and September 14, 1932, which are transcriptions of dialogue made after shooting was completed. Please note that the Paramount Story Files are housed in a collection distinct from the MPPDA Case Files.

7. Lamar Trotti to Hays, April 22, 1932, *Blonde Venus,* MPPDA Case Files, Academy Library.

8. Lamar Trotti, Memo, March 28, 1932, and Jason Joy to Hays, April 1, 1932, *Blonde Venus,* MPPDA Case Files, Academy Library.

9. Lamar Trotti to B. P. Schulberg, April 20, 1932, and Trotti to Hays, April 22, 1932, *Blonde Venus,* MPPDA Case Files, Academy Library.

10. Jason Joy to Hays, May 21, 1932, *Blonde Venus,* MPPDA Case Files, Academy Library.

11. Jason Joy to B. P. Schulberg, April 26, 1932, *Blonde Venus,* MPPDA Case Files, Academy Library.

12. Trotti to Hays, April 22, 1932, *Blonde Venus,* MPPDA Case Files, Academy Library.

13. Jason Joy to B. P. Schulberg, May 26, 1932, *Blonde Venus,* MPPDA Case Files, Academy Library.

14. Joy does, however, complain that the scene in which Helen takes the detective back to her boarding house is "boldly suggestive of an assignation," Joy to Schulberg, May 26, 1932, *Blonde Venus,* MPPDA Case Files, Academy Library.

15. Lamar Trotti, Memo, March 16, 1932, *Blonde Venus,* MPPDA Case Files, Academy Library.

16. For example, in the March (first) draft, scene C-10 opens with a description of the location of the club: "A side street in the neighborhood of Lenox Ave and 135th St; show the exterior of the MAGNOLIA CLUB. Colored children are playing in the street; colored men and women are passing by." In the same scene, O'Connor, the manager of the club, is talking to two "colored

girls" when Helen arrives with her agent, and his office is described as "covered with theatrical photographs, most of them young girls of all colors and in various stages of undress." In scene D-2, when Helen prepares to leave for her first performance, there is the following dialogue between her and Ned.

HELEN: The pianist promised to come early and go over my numbers with me. He's been perfectly darling to me.

NED (faking suspicion): He has, eh? Young fellow?

HELEN: Yes, dear. Young, big, strong, terribly good looking and very, very black.

See *Blonde Venus*, Paramount Story Files, Academy Library.

17. Joy to Schulberg, May 26, 1932, *Blonde Venus*, MPPDA Case Files, Academy Library.

18. Joy to Schulberg, May 26, 1932, *Blonde Venus*, MPPDA Case Files, Academy Library.

19. Compare the scene of Helen's trial in the final release print with the beginning of sequence "O" in the script dated March 18, 1932. *Blonde Venus*, Paramount Story Files, Academy Library.

20. In her analysis of *Blonde Venus*, E. Ann Kaplan says of Ned that "his dour presence throughout casts a pall on the supposedly ideal family with his essential meanness and his extreme, intolerant behavior," *Women and Film* 56. The problem with this kind of analysis, in my view, is that the description of character does not take account of the ways the film distorts conventional modes of characterization, both by refusing to motivate the story at this level and by setting up structural parallels between scenes (for example, the opening and closing versions of Helen and Ned's first meeting).

21. Lamar Trotti to B. P. Schulberg, April 20, 1932, *Blonde Venus*, MPPDA Case Files, Academy Library.

22. See for example Raymond Bellour, "L'évidence et le code" in *L'analyse du film* 123–30; an earlier version appeared in English in *Screen* 15, no. 4 (Winter 1974–75): 7–17; see also Janet Bergstrom's discussion of the concept of repetition in "Enunciation and Sexual Difference," *Camera Obscura* 3/4 (Summer 1979): 45. Analyzing the effects of repetition in terms of processes of cognition, David Bordwell argues that the classical Hollywood cinema favors redundancy as a means of permitting the viewer to form and verify hypotheses about story events. See Bordwell, Staiger, and Thompson, *Classical Hollywood Cinema* 31, and 43; Bordwell, *Narration in the Fiction Film* (Madison: University of Wisconsin Press, 1985), 56–57.

23. Jason Joy to Harold Hurley (Paramount Legal Department), September 1, 1932, and Joy to John Hammel (Paramount Distribution), September 16, 1932, *Blonde Venus*, MPPDA Case Files, Academy Library.

24. Joy to John Hammel, September 16, 1932, *Blonde Venus*, MPPDA Case Files, Academy Library.

25. *Confession*, Joe May, dir., Warners, 1937; *The House on 56th Street*, Robert Florey, dir., Warners, 1933; *The Sin of Madelon Claudet*, Edgar Selwyn, dir., MGM, 1931.

26. The distinction between narrative and spectacle was initially formulated by Laura Mulvey in an extremely influential discussion of how the Hollywood cinema mobilizes pleasure in looking: "Visual Pleasure and Narrative Cinema," *Screen*, 16, no. 3 (Autumn 1975): 6–18. Mulvey takes Sternberg's films as weighted heavily toward spectacle, an organization of space which fixes the woman as fetishized object of the male gaze. She argues that in spectacle, the diegetic world of the narrative "fades" and identification with character is broken off in favor of a direct erotic rapport between the image and the spectator. The psychoanalytic concepts Mulvey invokes suggest that this spectator's position is a highly if not exclusively masculine one. In contrast to Mulvey, I argue that there are certain filiations between narrative and spectacle in *Blonde Venus*. The diegetic world of the narrative does not entirely fade away. Also, I am setting aside the problem of gendered spectatorship for the moment, to consider how the spectator is led to comprehend or interpret the love affair (a conscious process which I do not take to be sexually differentiated).

5. The Production Code Administration's Policies and Procedures

1. The films are listed in a memo, Joseph Breen to Hays, February 20, 1935, *Baby Face*, MPPDA Case Files, Academy Library.

2. Joseph Breen, Annual Report, dated March 1, 1936, and covering the year 1935, in the files of the Motion Picture Producers and Distributors Association, Los Angeles. Breen writes: "In addition to the routine work with source materials and scripts, as well as the final review of the picture, the Production Code Administration during 1935 was called upon to examine 412 pictures which were produced and released prior to July 15, 1934, the day on which the formal certification of approval by the Production Code Administration was made mandatory. Due to the wide spread practice of double billing, a substantial number of these old pictures were reissued for general exhibition, which made it necessary for the Production Code Administration to examine all such pictures before issuing certificates of approval." Breen's annual reports included lists of scripts the Production Code Administration considered unsuitable or problematic, and, for the reports dated 1935 and 1936, discussion of censorship policy and procedure.

3. Throughout 1933 and 1934 Hays received biweekly accounts of the publicity that was being directed against the industry. The remark about the "state of war" is from one such report, dated October 14, 1934, Hays Collection, Indiana State Library.

4. From the perspective of educational psychology, a number of the Payne Fund Studies take up the question of the extent to which behavior and attitudes could be shaped by the movies. These include: George D. Stoddard, *Getting Ideas from the Movies* (New York: Macmillan, 1933); Frank K. Shuttleworth and Mark A. May, *The Social Conduct and Attitudes of Movie Fans* (New York: Macmillan, 1933); Ruth Peterson and L. L. Thurstone, *Motion Pictures and the Social Attitudes of Children* (New York: Macmillan, 1933). Two studies focus on the physiological effects of film viewing: Wendell S. Dysinger and Christian A. Ruckmick, *The Emotional Responses of Children to the Motion Picture Situation* (New York: Macmillan, 1935); Samuel Renshaw, Vernon L. Miller, and Dorothy F. Marquis, *Children's Sleep* (New York: Macmillan, 1933). Herbert Blumer's *Motion Pictures and Conduct* (New York: Macmillan, 1933) is concerned with the ways in which film engages instinctual drives and processes of fantasy.

5. Werrett Wallace Charters, *Motion Pictures and Youth* (New York: Macmillan, 1933), 31–41.

6. A somewhat skeptical review of Henry James Forman's *Our Movie Made Children* (New York: Macmillan, 1935) may be found in the *Saturday Review of Literature*, July 22, 1933. *Parent's Magazine* devoted two articles to the research, both by James Rorty: "New Facts about Movies and Children" (July 1933) and "How Movies Harm Children" (August 1933). Various journals of education also referred to the studies: H. G. Campbell, "Moving Pictures and School Children," *School and Society* 39 (June 30, 1934); C. C. Peters, "The Relation of Motion Pictures to Standards of Morality," *School and Society* 39 (March 31, 1934); and in a title indicative of the general hysteria of the time, F. Peterson, "Germs that Attack the Mind," *Education* 55 (November 1934).

7. The series published in the *Christian Century* is as follows: "Your Child and the Movies" (May 3, 1933); "The Movies and Your Child's Health" (May 19, 1933); "The Movies and Your Child's Emotions" (May 17, 1933); "The Movies and Your Child's Conduct" (May 24, 1933); "The Movies and Delinquency" (May 31, 1933); "Movies and Our Neighbors' Children" (June 7, 1933); "What Can We Do about the Movies?" (June 14, 1933).

8. The MPPDA reports concerning negative publicity are listed by date in the Hays Collection, Indiana State Library. The reports indicate that Hays was well aware of the way the Payne Fund research was being used against the industry. One report, dated May 2, 1933, is entitled "Introducing the 'Big Noise' Team— Eastman and Short" and explains that Fred Eastman is to write the series of articles that was eventually published in the *Christian Century*. In the report of December 5, 1933, several advance reviews of Henry James Forman's *Our*

Movie Made Children are discussed. In the report of May 31, 1933, it was noted that Forman was giving speeches derived from his book, "indicting the movies."

9. Report of May 2, 1933, Hays Collection, Indiana State Library.

10. Raymond Moley, *Are We Movie Made?* (New York: Macy-Masius, 1938).

11. Memo, Breen to Hays, March 2, 1933, Hays Collection, Indiana State Library.

12. Alice Ames Winter to Hays, November 21, 1933, Hays Collection, Indiana State Library.

13. Hays refers to having seen *Baby Face*, in a memo, April 20, 1933, *Baby Face*, MPPDA Case Files, Academy Library.

14. Alice Ames Winter writes to Hays: "The set up for which you provided before you left was intended, as I understand, to create a balance between the work for the general flavor of pictures, represented by the type of mind that Colonel Joy gives to problems, and the narrower considerations of the censor point of view that Doctor Wingate contributes," November 21, 1933, Hays Collection, Indiana State Library.

15. Will Hays, Memo, January 6, 1934, Hays Collection, Indiana State Library.

16. Hays to Maurice McKenzie, January 5, 1934, Hays Collection, Indiana State Library.

17. The reports on publicity contained in the Hays Collection indicate that publicity devoted to the Legion did not begin to build until late January of 1934, and the peak of the campaign, the threatened boycott, was not discussed in the daily press until June.

18. Despite the importance usually ascribed to it, a detailed social history of the Legion of Decency remains to be written. For more on the film industry's relationship with the Catholic Church see Richard Maltby, *Reforming the Movies: Hollywood, the Hays Office, and the Campaign for Film Censorship, 1908–1938* (Oxford University Press, forthcoming).

19. Fred Beetson to Hays, February 15, 1934, Hays Collection, Indiana State Library.

20. Vizzard, *See No Evil* 33–37.

21. Paul Facey, *The Legion of Decency: A Sociological Analysis of the Emergence and Development of a Social Pressure Group* (New York: Arno Press, 1974), 39.

22. Thus, for example, in a report to Hays of February 14, 1934, Bishop Cantwell quotes the Code against the industry, Hays Collection, Indiana State Library.

23. Breen, Annual Report, dated February 15, 1935, and covering the year 1934, in the files of the Motion Picture Producers and Distributors Association, Los Angeles. Breen lists the men working under him as follows: James Wingate,

Geoffrey Shurlock, Islin Auster, Douglas MacKinnon, Carl Lischka, Arthur Houghton, John Stewart, and Vincent Hart. He states: "With the increase in personnel, it is now possible for the Production Code Administration to follow more closely the day by day activity in the production of the pictures."

24. Breen, Annual Report, dated February 15, 1935, and covering the year 1934, in the files of the MPPDA, Los Angeles.

25. MPPDA press release of June 22, 1934, in the Hays Collection, Indiana State Library.

26. For an example of Breen discussing what the boards are likely to pass, see Breen to Jack Warner, March 18, 1939, *The Old Maid*, MPPDA Case Files, Academy Library.

27. Annual Report, dated March 15, 1936, and covering the year 1935, in the files of the MPPDA, Los Angeles.

28. Annual Report, dated February 15, 1935, and covering the year 1934, in the files of the MPPDA, Los Angeles.

29. Annual Report, dated March 15, 1936, and covering the year 1935, in the files of the MPPDA, Los Angeles.

30. Breen to Daryl Zanuck, n.d., *Private Number*, MPPDA Case Files, Academy Library.

31. William Everson suggests that it is only after 1938, once the worst of the public relations crisis had passed, that the Production Code Administration relaxed its requirements in the treatment of screwball. See "Screwball Comedy, A Reappraisal," *Films in Review* (December 1983): 582.

32. Breen to Luigi Luraschi, November 17, 1941, *Palm Beach Story*, MPPDA Case Files, Academy Library.

33. From Mrs. S. Vincius, Amusement Inspector, City of San Antonio, March 28, 1941, *The Lady Eve*; from Mrs. John Degnan, April 18, 1944, *The Miracle of Morgan's Creek*; Carl Milliken writes to Breen of further protests, March 7, 1944; *The Miracle of Morgan's Creek*, MPPDA Case Files, Academy Library.

34. Thomas Brahan, editorial, *Chattanooga Tennessee Times*, November 30, 1941, *Two-Faced Woman*, MPPDA Case Files, Academy Library.

35. Annual Report, dated March 15, 1936, and covering the year 1935, in the files of the MPPDA, Los Angeles.

36. Ibid.

37. Breen to Louis B. Mayer, December 21, 1934, *Anna Karenina*, MPPDA Case Files, Academy Library.

38. Breen to Hays, October 7, 1935, *Anna Karenina*, MPPDA Case Files, Academy Library.

39. Breen to Hays, October 14, 1935, *Anna Karenina*, MPPDA Case Files, Academy Library.

40. Annual Report, dated March 15, 1936, and covering the year 1935, in the files of the MPPDA, Los Angeles.

41. Breen seems to have explicitly required that the scene be played so that whatever has occurred during the elided time while Anna is alone with Vronsky in his flat remains ambiguous or hard to interpret. He cautions the producer: "The use of a *sofa* in this scene is inadvisable. The scene as a whole should be toned down, to avoid the present suggestion of a previous passionate episode between them. The following lines should be deleted or changed: 'I have nobody in the world but you now, dear—remember that!' " Breen to David Selznick, March 5, 1935, *Anna Karenina,* MPPDA Case Files, Academy Library.

42. Annual Report, dated March 15, 1936, and covering the year 1935, in the files of the MPPDA, Los Angeles.

43. Ibid.

44. Ibid.

45. In a discussion of *Stagecoach,* Nick Browne discusses the way in which point of view can become charged with moral significance. See "The Spectator-in-the-Text: The Rhetoric of Stagecoach," in *The Rhetoric of Filmic Narration* (Michigan: UMI Research Press, 1982).

46. Annual Report, dated March 15, 1936, and covering the year 1935, in the files of the MPPDA, Los Angeles.

47. Ibid.

48. The dialogue between Anna and Vronsky is as follows:

ANNA: I feel pain, I feel tears.

VRONSKY: Why?

ANNA: Because I am so happy. Not to think, not to believe, only to feel. . . . We'll be punished.

VRONSKY: Punished?

ANNA: For being so happy.

49. Breen to Maurice Rivar of Universal Studios, March 29, 1940, *Back Street,* MPPDA Case Files, Academy Library.

6. *Class and Glamour in the Films of the Late Thirties*

1. Breen, Internal Memo, May 16, 1936, *Camille,* MPPDA Case Files, Academy Library.

2. [Breen], Unsigned Letter to Samuel Goldwyn, November 30, 1931, *The Greeks Had a Word for Them,* MPPDA Case Files, Academy Library. I conclude the letter was written by Breen on basis of its style and also a résumé of November 25, in which it is noted that he viewed a print with Hays.

3. Breen to Hays, June 8, 1933, *Baby Face,* MPPDA Case Files, Academy Library.

4. See E. Ann Kaplan, "The Case of the Missing Mother: Maternal Issues in Vidor's *Stella Dallas,*" *Heresies* 16 (1983): 81–85; Williams, " 'Something Else Besides a Mother,' " *Cinema Journal* 24, no. 1 (Fall 1984): 2–27; and the

exchange in *Cinema Journal* 25, no. 1 (Fall 1985): 50–54 and no. 4 (Summer 1986): 44–53.

5. The line is a reference to drinking in a scene in which Stella is observed in the company of Ed Munn, and appears to be drinking alcohol. *Stella Dallas*, MPPDA Case Files, Academy Library.

6. Williams, " 'Something Else,' " 16–23.

7. Synopsis dated September 13, 1939, *Kitty Foyle*, RKO Story Files, RKO Archive, Los Angeles.

8. Breen to Joseph Nolan, March 27, 1940, *Kitty Foyle*, MPPDA Case Files, Academy Library.

9. That this was of great concern to Breen is evident in his letter to Nolan, July 15, 1940: "It will also be necessary to indicate that Kitty's child, born in the hospital, is the offspring of her *legitimate marriage* to Wyn, even though it is indicated that this marriage has been annulled. The point, here, is to make certain that there be no doubt as to the legitimacy of the child," *Kitty Foyle*, MPPDA Case Files, Academy Library.

10. Breen to Joseph Nolan, July 15, 1940, *Kitty Foyle*, MPPDA Case Files, Academy Library.

11. Breen to Joseph Nolan, March 27, 1940, *Kitty Foyle*, MPPDA Case Files, Academy Library.

12. First Draft, by Donald Ogden Stewart, dated April 30, 1940, and Second Draft, by Dalton Trumbo, dated July 10, 1940, *Kitty Foyle*, RKO Story Files, RKO Archive, Los Angeles.

13. I have not found any correspondence in which Breen recommends any specific alterations along these lines to the producers. It is possible that the changes effected in the screenplay are the result of verbal agreements between Breen and the studio. Or they may have been entirely an invention of the screenwriters, attempting to render a difficult story acceptable to the Production Code Administration. Whatever their origin, the point is that during the process of revising the script, elements were introduced which serve a compensatory function and clearly fit Breen's definition of compensating moral values.

14. In this regard it is interesting that one of the studio producers who originally gave approval on this project assesses its potential appeal in terms of the relationship between the "white collar girl" and the wealthy man. That is, the producer is interested in precisely those elements that censorship seeks to deny or negate: "What we do think we are getting and will have in this picture, in addition to the interest of the love affairs, is—underneath it all—the tone of a Cinderella story, which the book definitely calls for, and I think is one of the big charms of this story." Harry Edington to George J. Schaefer, August 15, 1940, *Kitty Foyle*, RKO Production Files, RKO Archive, Los Angeles.

15. *American Cinematographer*, January 1941: 32.

16. Raymond Bellour, "Le blocage symbolique," in *L'analyse du film*, 131–246; Stephen Heath, "Film, System, Narrative," in *Questions of Cinema* (London: Macmillan, 1981), 131–44.

7. Afterword

1. For example, Sklar, *Movie-Made America* 175. He writes: "In the first half decade of the Great Depression, Hollywood's movie-makers perpetrated one of the most remarkable challenges to traditional values in the history of mass commercial entertainment. The movies called into question sexual propriety, social decorum and the institutions of law and order."

BIBLIOGRAPHY

Unpublished Sources

Catholic Legion of Decency. "Motion Pictures Classified by the National Legion of Decency, February 1936–November 1948." A comprehensive list of the Legion's ratings of films for the period. Library of Performing Arts, New York Public Library, New York, N.Y.

Hays Collection. Hays's correspondence filed by date. Special Collections, Indiana State Library, Indianapolis, Indiana.

MGM Story Files. Includes scripts and treatments for only selected titles. Special Collections, Doheny Library, University of Southern California, Los Angeles.

Motion Picture Producers and Distributors Association. Annual Reports dated 1935 and 1936. Private correspondence from Joseph Breen to Will Hays, which should be distinguished from the *Annual Reports* that the MPPDA published and distributed in pamphlet form. Motion Picture Producers Association, Los Angeles, Calif.

Motion Picture Producers and Distributors Association. Censorship Case Files. Covers the years 1928–68. Includes correspondence, lists of cuts made by state and foreign censor boards, and letters of complaint from reform groups. Margaret Herrick Library, Academy of Motion Picture Arts and Sciences, Beverly Hills, Calif.

Paramount Story Files. Extensive collection of scripts and treatments. Margaret Herrick Library, Academy of Motion Picture Arts and Sciences, Beverly Hills, Calif.

RKO Story and Legal Files. Story files contain scripts, treatments, and some intrastudio correspondence; legal files contain correspondence relating to censorship. RKO Archive, Los Angeles, Calif.

United Artists Collection. Warner Brothers Press Books. Press kits designed by the studio for distribution to exhibitors. State Historical Society, Madison, Wis.

Warner Brothers Story and Production Files. Story files contain scripts and treatments; production files contain correspondence relating to censorship. Special Collections, Doheny Library, University of Southern California, Los Angeles, Calif.

Published Sources

Albrecht, Donald. *Designing Dreams: Modern Architecture in the Movies*. New York: Harper & Row, 1986.

Auerbach, Nina. *Woman and the Demon: The Life of a Victorian Myth*. Cambridge: Harvard University Press, 1982.

Baym, Nina. *Women's Fiction: A Guide to Novels by and about Women in America, 1820–1870*. Ithaca: Cornell University Press, 1978.

Bergman, Andrew. *We're in the Money: Depression America and Its Films*. New York: Harper, 1971.

Bergstrom, Janet. "Enunciation and Sexual Difference, (Part I)." Camera Obscura 3/4 (1979): 33–65.

Bergstrom, Janet. "Rereading the Work of Claire Johnston." *Camera Obscura* 3/4 (1979): 21–32.

Blumer, Herbert, and Philip M. Hauser. *Movies, Delinquency, and Crime*. New York: Macmillan, 1933.

Bordwell, David, Janet Staiger, and Kristin Thompson. *The Hollywood Classical Cinema: Film Style and Mode of Production to 1960*. New York: Columbia, 1985.

Cahiers du Cinéma. "John Ford's *Young Mr. Lincoln*." July/Aug 1970. Reprinted in *Movies and Methods*, vol. 1, ed. Bill Nichols. Berkeley: University of California Press, 1976.

Cahiers du Cinéma. "Morocco." Nov/Dec 1970. Translated in *Sternberg*, ed. Peter Baxter. London: BFI Publishing, 1980.

Campbell, Marilyn. "RKO's Fallen Women, 1930–1933." *Velvet Light Trap*, no. 10 (Fall 1973): 13–16.

Carmen, Ira. *Movies, Censorship, and the Law*. Ann Arbor: University of Michigan Press, 1967.

Charters, Werrett Wallace. *Motion Pictures and Youth*. New York: Macmillan, 1933.

Comolli, Jean-Louis, and Jean Narboni. "Cinema/Ideology/Criticism." *Cahiers du Cinéma*, Oct/Nov 1969. Translated in *Screen* 12, no. 1 (Spring 1971): 27–36.

Conant, Michael. *Antitrust in the Motion Picture Industry*. Berkeley: University of California Press, 1960.

Cott, Nancy F. "Passionlessness: An Interpretation of Victorian Sexual Ideology, 1790–1850." *Signs* 4, no. 2 (Winter 1978): 219–36.

Dale, Edgar. *The Content of Motion Pictures*. New York: Macmillan, 1935.

de Cordova, Richard. "The Emergence of the Star System in America: An Examination of the Institutional and Ideological Function of the Star: 1907–1922." Diss., University of California, Los Angeles, 1986.

Eckert, Charles. "The Carole Lombard in Macy's Window." *Quarterly Review of Film Studies* 3, no. 1 (Winter 1978): 1–21.

Elsaesser, Thomas. "Tales of Sound and Fury: Observations on the Family Melodrama." *Monogram* 4 (1972). Reprinted in *Home Is Where the Heart Is: Studies in Melodrama and the Woman's Film*, ed. Christine Gledhill. London: British Film Institute, 1987.

Everson, William. "Screwball Comedy, A Reappraisal." *Films in Review*, December 1983: 578–84.

Facey, Paul. *The Legion of Decency: A Sociological Analysis of the Emergence and Development of a Social Pressure Group*. Diss., Fordham University, 1945. New York: Arno Press, 1974.

Forman, Henry James. *Our Movie Made Children*. New York: Macmillan, 1935.

Forty, Adrian. *Objects of Desire: Design and Society from Wedgwood to IBM*. New York: Pantheon, 1986.

Foucault, Michel. *The History of Sexuality, Vol. 1: An Introduction*. Trans. Robert Hurley. New York: Vintage Books, 1978.

Garrison, Dee. "Immoral Fiction in the Late Victorian Library." *American Quarterly* 28, no. 1 (Spring 1976): 71–89.

Gay, Peter. *Education of the Senses*, vol. 1 of *The Bourgeois Experience: Victoria to Freud*. Oxford: Oxford University Press, 1984.

Gebhard, David. "The Moderne in the U.S. 1920–1941." *Architectural Association Quarterly* 2 (1970): 4–20.

Griffith, Richard. "Cycles and Genres." An additional section of the book *The Film Till Now*, by Paul Rotha. London: Vision Press, 1949.

Haight, Anne Lyon. *Banned Books: 387 B.C. to 1978 A.D.* Updated and enlarged by Chandler B. Grannis. New York: R. R. Bowker, 1978.

Hambley, John, and Patrick Downing. *The Art of Hollywood: A Thames Television Exhibition at the Victoria and Albert Museum*. London: Macdermott & Chant, 1979.

Haralovich, Mary Beth. "The Mandates of Good Taste: The Self-Regulation of Film Advertising in the Thirties." *Wide Angle* 6, no. 2 (1984): 50–57.

Haralovich, Mary Beth. "Motion Picture Advertising: Industrial and Social Forces and Effects." Diss., University of Wisconsin–Madison, 1984.

Hays, Will. *Memoirs*. New York: Doubleday, 1955.

Hillier, Bevis. *The World of Art Deco*. Catalogue for an exhibition organized by the Minneapolis Institute of the Arts. New York: E. P. Dutton, 1971.

Huettig, Mae D. *Economic Control of the Motion Picture Industry: A Study in Industrial Organization*. Philadelphia: University of Pennsylvania Press, 1944.

Inglis, Ruth A. *Freedom of the Movies: A Report from the Commission on Freedom of the Press*. Chicago: University of Chicago Press, 1947.

Johnston, Claire. "Women's Cinema as Counter Cinema." In *Movies and Methods*, vol. 1, ed. Bill Nichols. Los Angeles: University of California Press, 1976.

Jowett, Garth. *Film: The Democratic Art*. Boston: Little, Brown, 1976.

Kaplan, E. Ann. "The Case of the Missing Mother: Maternal Issues in Vidor's *Stella Dallas*." *Heresies* 16 (1983): 81–85.

Kaplan, E. Ann. "Mothering, Feminism, and Representation: The Maternal in Melodrama and the Woman's Film, 1910–40." In *Home Is Where the Heart Is: Studies in Melodrama and the Woman's Film*, ed. Christine Gledhill. London: British Film Institute, 1987.

Kaplan, E. Ann. *Women and Film: Both Sides of the Camera*. New York: Methuen, 1983.

Klinger, Barbara. "Cinema/Ideology/Criticism Revisited: The Progressive Text." *Screen* 25, no. 1 (January/February 1984): 30–44.

Koppes, Clayton R., and Gregory D. Black. *Hollywood Goes to War: How Politics, Profits, and Propaganda Shaped World War II Movies*. New York: Macmillan, 1987.

Kuhn, Annette. *Cinema, Censorship, and Sexuality, 1909–1925*. London: Routledge, 1988.

Kuhn, Annette. *The Power of the Image: Essays on Representation and Sexuality*. London: Routledge & Kegan Paul, 1985.

LaCapra, Dominick. *Madame Bovary on Trial*. Ithaca: Cornell University Press, 1982.

Leff, Leonard J., and Jerold L. Simmons. *The Dame in the Kimono: Hollywood, Censorship, and the Production Code from the 1920s to the 1960s*. New York: Grove Weidenfeld, 1990.

Lister, Raymond. *Victorian Narrative Painting*. New York: C. N. Potter, 1966.

McLane, Betsy Ann. "Hollywood's Fallen Women Features." Masters Thesis, University of Southern California, 1978.

Maltby, Richard. " 'Baby Face' or How Joe Breen Made Barbara Stanwyck Atone for Causing the Wall Street Crash." *Screen* 27, no. 2 (March/April 1986): 22–45.

Maltby, Richard. *Reforming the Movies: Hollywood, the Hays Office, and the Campaign for Film Censorship, 1908–1938*. Oxford University Press, forthcoming.

Mandelbaum, Howard, and Eric Myers. *Screen Deco: A Celebration of High Style in Hollywood*. New York: St. Martin's Press, 1985.

May, Lary. *Screening Out the Past: The Birth of Mass Culture and the Motion Picture Industry*. Oxford: Oxford University Press, 1980.

Mitchell, Sally. *The Fallen Angel: Chastity, Class, and Women's Reading, 1835–1880*. Bowling Green, Ohio: Bowling Green University Popular Press, 1981.

Moley, Raymond. *Are We Movie Made?* New York: Macy-Masius, 1938.

Moley, Raymond. *The Hays Office*. New York: Bobbs Merrill, 1945.

Mulvey, Laura. "Visual Pleasure and Narrative Cinema." *Screen* 16, no. 3 (Autumn 1975): 6–18.

Nochlin, Linda. "Lost and *Found:* Once More the Fallen Woman." *Art Bulletin* 60 (1978): 141–44.

Petro, Patrice. *Joyless Streets: Women and Melodramatic Representation in Weimar Germany.* Princeton: Princeton University Press, 1989.

Quigley, Martin. *Decency in Motion Pictures.* New York: Macmillan, 1937.

Seydel, Renate, and Allan Hagedorff, eds. *Asta Nielsen: Ihr Leben in Fotodokumenten, Selbstzeugnissen und zeitgenössischen Betrachtungen.* Munich: Universitas Verlag, 1981.

Shenton, Herbert. *The Public Relations of the Motion Picture Industry.* New York: Federal Council of Churches of Christ in America, 1931; rpt. New York: Jerome S. Ozer, 1971.

Sklar, Robert. *Movie-Made America: How the Movies Changed American Life.* New York: Random House, 1975.

Sternberg, Joseph von. *Fun in a Chinese Laundry.* New York: Macmillan, 1965.

Thompson, Kristin. *Exporting Entertainment: America in the World Film Market, 1907–1934.* London: British Film Institute, 1985.

Viviani, Christian. "Who Is without Sin? The Maternal Melodrama in American Film, 1930–1939." *Wide Angle* 4, no. 2 (1980): 4–17.

Vizzard, Jack. *See No Evil: Life inside a Hollywood Censor.* New York: Simon and Schuster, 1971.

Wall, James M. "Oral History with Geoffrey Shurlock." ts., Louis B. Mayer Library, American Film Institute, Los Angeles. A.F.I., 1975.

Watt, George. *The Fallen Woman in the Nineteenth-Century Novel.* Totowa, N.J.: Barnes and Noble, 1984.

Welter, Barbara. "The Cult of True Womanhood: 1820–1860." *American Quarterly* 18 (Summer 1966): 151–74.

Williams, Linda. " 'Something Else besides a Mother': *Stella Dallas* and the Maternal Melodrama." *Cinema Journal* 24, no. 1 (Fall 1984): 2–27.

INDEX

Films are entered in this index by title, each title being followed by country of production (if not the United States), production company (and distributor, if different), and year of release. Literary works are entered by author's name, and followed by an indication of genre where this is not the novel.

Chanel of Paris, 63
Charters, Werrett Wallace, director of
Payne Fund Studies, 107, 180
Chase, Rev. William Sheaf, director of
Federal Motion Picture Council, 171
chastity, ideal of, 8, 165
Chattanooga Tennessee Times, The, 182
Christian Century, The (magazine), 31,
107, 180
Cinderella story, 11–13, 58–59,
141–43, 145–46, 149, 166, 184
cinema audience: children, 10, 107;
delinquents, 107, 163–64; effect of
films on, 83, 99, 107, 109, 118;
immigrants, 10, 17, 107; teenage
girls, 10, 17, 133, 137, 163–64;
women, 3–4
Claire, Ina, 63
Clarke, Donald Henderson: *Female,* 10
classical Hollywood film, the, xi, 24, 79,
94, 125, 133, 148–49, 178, 185
Classified (Corinne Griffiths
Productions/First National, 1925), 12
Cohn, Harry, of Columbia, 3, 163
Collins, Wilkie: *Fallen Leaves, The,* 7;
New Magdalen, The, 7
Colton, John, co-author of *Rain*
(play), 9
Columbia Pictures Corporation, 3, 30,
169–70
comedy, film, 66–70, 73–74, 82–83,
157; screwball, 113, 157, 182
Comolli, Jean-Louis, 168
compensating moral values, rule of,
40–42, 45–46, 48–50, 70, 76–78,
88, 92–95, 104, 115, 118–21, 133,
138, 140–42, 148
Comstock, Anthony, head of the New
York Society for the Suppression of
Vice, 166
Conant, Michael, 28, 169
Confession (Warner Brothers, 1937), 95,
179
consumer goods in films, 13, 16–17,
44–45, 56–57, 63, 133
costume, film, 56–60, 62–64, 112,
124, 133, 143

Cott, Nancy F., 165
courtesan, the, 7, 52, 95

Dale, Edgar, author of Payne Fund
Studies, 16, 167
Dance, Girl, Dance (RKO, 1940), 168
de Cordova, Richard, 169
decor, film, 53–56, 62, 64, 84, 112,
124, 133, 143
Degnan, Mrs. John, complainant to
MPPDA, 182
delinquency: male, 5, 17; female, 4–5, 17
Depinet, Ned, of RKO, 175
Department of Moral Welfare of US
Presbyterian Church, 171
Depression, Great, The, 12–13, 70,
166, 175, 185
Dey, Richard, set designer, 53
Dietrich, Marlene, 85, 87, 91, 100–102
director, art, the, 53
Don'ts and Be Carefuls, list issued by
the MPPDA (1927), 28, 170
Downing, Patrick, 173
Dreiser, Theodore: *American Tragedy,
An,* 170; *Sister Carrie,* 8–9, 166
Dumas, Alexandre: *La Dame aux
camélias,* 7, 11, 41
Ďurovičová, Nataša, xii
Dysinger, Wendell S., author of Payne
Fund Study, 180

Easiest Way, The (Clara Kimball Young
Film/Selznick Pictures, 1917), 172
Easiest Way, The (MGM, 1931), 36,
42–52, 56, 57 fig. 3.4, 58 fig. 3.5,
59, 59 fig. 3.6, 60, 60 fig. 3.7, 90,
115, 135, 151–52, 171–74
East Is West (Universal, 1930), 171
East Lynne (Fox, 1916), 11
East Lynne (Hugo Ballin Productions/
W. W. Hodkinson, 1921), 11
East Lynne (Fox, 1931), 11
Eastman, Fred, contributor to *Christian
Century,* 180
Easy Living (Paramount, 1937), 57–58
Eckert, Charles, 57, 62, 174
Edington, Harry, of RKO, 166, 184